CHELMSFORD
A HISTORY

Half Moon Inn during the snow storms of 1881.

CHELMSFORD
A HISTORY

David Jones

Phillimore

2003

Published by
PHILLIMORE & CO. LTD
Shopwyke Manor Barn, Chichester, West Sussex

ISBN 1 86077 246 3

Printed and bound in Great Britain by
THE CROMWELL PRESS
Trowbridge, Wiltshire

To Jill
and to Toby,
Jessica and Chloe

Messages to Chelmsford's twinned towns:

France: Annonay – Veuillez recevoir nos chaleureuses pensées de la part votre ville jumelée

Germany: Backnang – Die herzlichsten Grüssen an unsere Partnerstadt

Contents

List of Illustrations

Frontispiece: Half Moon Inn, 1881

Acknowledgements

Anyone writing about the history of Chelmsford is conscious of those who have already published work on the subject. Chief among these is the late Hilda Grieve, whose two-volume history, *The Sleepers and the Shadows*, is the standard work on the town between the Norman Conquest and the formation of the Borough Council in 1888. Her books are an almost inexhaustible supply of detailed information and I acknowledge a very great debt to her. Many others have contributed significantly to our knowledge, among them Nancy Briggs, Stan Jarvis, John Marriage and the late Gilbert Torry, and I am grateful to them for the benefit of their meticulously researched publications.

My sincere thanks are due to Nick Wickenden for reading parts of the text and to Ronald Bond for reading the rest. Their advice and guidance have been invaluable. Any mistakes which remain are my own. I am grateful to Nick, too, in his capacity as Museums Manager and to his colleagues Dot Bedenham, Ann Lutyens-Humphry and Ian Hook for their kind assistance and encouragement. I would also like to express my gratitude to Geoff Liggett who has not only been good enough to loan postcards from his collection but has also provided original photographs plus humour, support and calm reassurance. Pete Rogers has produced many of the photographs and I am most grateful to him.

I am happy to acknowledge my thanks to the following for their kind permission to use illustrations and quotations: Chelmsford Museum (Chelmsford Borough Council), cover illustration, frontispiece, 1, 4, 5-17, 19-23, 25, 29-31, 37-40, 42, 47, 48, 51, 53-60, 63-5, 67-73, 80, 83-94, 97, 98, 100, 101, 103, 105-8, 112, 114, 117, 120, 124, 127-9, 135, 139, 140, 142-4, 146; Colchester Museums, 33; Essex Record office, 26-8, 34, 43; Essex County Council, 2, 3; Geoff Liggett, 32, 35, 36, 44-6, 49, 50, 66, 74-9, 82, 95, 96, 99, 102, 104, 109, 110-11, 115-16, 115, 118-19, 122, 123, 125-6, 130-4, 136-7, 141, 147-149; Arthur Wright, AMA, FRSA, 61, 62; Derek Wilks, 41, 49, 113, 121, 138; Prue James, 81 and wording for caption 145; the Head and Governors of Moulsham High School, 24; the *Essex Chronicle*, 18, 52; Yale University Press, for quotation from *Buildings of England: Essex* by Nikolaus Pevsner (originally published by Penguin Books); Helen Walker, 145.

Introduction

Chelmsford is happy in possessing little in the way of history and is chiefly known as an important agricultural centre.

Essex Business Review, 1888-90.

Chelmsford lies at the very heart of the county of Essex and has been the county town for eight hundred years. Its geographical position has marked it, from the Roman period, as the hub of the area, an important place either in itself or on the way to others, notably London, Colchester and Southend on Sea.

For most of its existence, Chelmsford has been an agricultural and market town but the Assizes enhanced its status as a place to visit. Later it became an industrial focus attracting Crompton, Hoffmann and Marconi, the last establishing the first radio factory in the world and making Chelmsford the birthplace of radio.

In more recent times, the town's location has increased its importance as a commuter community and considerable residential and commercial development resulted in its rapid expansion in the last quarter of the 20th century. This expansion has subsumed the neighbouring hamlet of Moulsham and drawn in Springfield, Broomfield, Writtle, the Baddows and others.

This history can only give a broad outline of Chelmsford's progress and much must be omitted including the story of its satellites. What it does hope to achieve is to recount the development of a community of, as the coat of arms states, 'Many Minds – One Heart'.

One

The Site and Beginnings of Chelmsford

Chelmsford Hundred lies in the heart of the County; and, besides the convenience of situation, has many and great advantages above most of the rest. The land in general is very good …

The History and Antiquities of Essex
Philip Morant, 1768

The area of the Borough of Chelmsford consists of gently undulating landscape dissected by river valleys. Generally the land slopes from the north-west to the south-east and its geology is dominated by the effects of the last ice age. Chelmsford marks the southern margin of the maximum ice extent. Wright's *History of Essex* describes the soil as being 'principally a deep rich loam, intermixed with veins of gravel'. This and the drainage patterns have influenced the type of cultivation and animal husbandry followed in the area. Much of the surroundings of Chelmsford is still farming-based and has suffered from intensive agriculture and the use of fertilisers and pesticides, but the wealth of different habitat provided by man's hand still

1 Chelmsford from the gravel pits at Springfield Hill, 1831, from Wright's *History and Topography of the County of Essex*.

1

2 Reconstruction of the Neolithic cursus at Springfield from an original watercolour by Frank Gardiner.

allows a diversity of wildlife. Ancient woodland, grassland, heath and river valleys are supplemented by coppice, hedgerow, ponds, lakes, gardens and churchyards.

There is no evidence of early human activity at the confluence of Chelmsford's two rivers, the Can and the Chelmer, although evidence has suggested there may have been a small number of late Iron-Age round-houses on the corner of Parkway and Moulsham Street at the time of the Roman invasion. The earliest settlement in the district was on the site of Chelmer village, where a Neolithic cursus, a ceremonial monument, was established *c*.2000 B.C. The cursus, which was discovered by aerial photography, ran approximately from Barnes Farm roundabout to the Asda car park.

Fertile land in the area would have seen the establishment of many small farmsteads in the river valleys during the Bronze Age from *c*.1500 B.C. onwards. An excavation at Springfield Lyons has revealed a circular ditched enclosure dating from *c*.850 B.C., which may have been the defended home of a local chief.

3 Reconstruction of the Bronze-Age circular enclosure at Springfield Lyons from an original watercolour by Frank Gardiner.

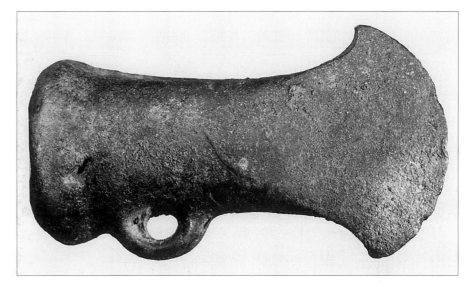

4 Bronze-Age socketed axe-head.

Among the finds were thousands of clay moulds used in the manufacture of bronze swords and other weapons. In the Iron Age, a hill fort was established at Danbury and, at Little Waltham, a village grew up, discovered and later excavated because of the cutting of the Little Waltham bypass in the early 1970s.

When the four legions and auxiliary troops of the Roman emperor Claudius arrived in Britain in A.D. 43, the army proceeded immediately towards Colchester, Camulodunum, to establish Roman authority at the tribal capital of the Essex tribe, the Trinovantes, and capital of virtually the whole of south-eastern Britain. His men would have passed through the area of Chelmsford but pottery analysis of excavated sites has shown that no settlement was established until after the defeat of Boudicca, the queen of the Norfolk tribe, the Iceni, who revolted against Roman power. The harsh brutality of the Roman invaders had resulted in the flogging of Boudicca and the ravishing of her daughters. The Trinovantes, who joined the revolt, had also suffered from the occupier's arrogance, losing land at Colchester to Roman colonists who merely helped themselves and

evicted the existing owners. Boudicca and her allies were decisively defeated in A.D. 61, having first sacked Colchester, London and St Albans and caused 70,000 deaths, according to the official figures quoted by Tacitus.

There was never to be a repeat of Boudicca's revolt, probably because of the setting up of small forts like the one at Chelmsford, built on the now established road from London to Colchester and about a day's march from each of them. The fort, which also commanded the strategic river crossing, lasted only about ten years, giving way to the civilian settlement of Caesaromagus, 'Caesar's Market'. It had the distinction of being the only town in Roman Britain to be given the imperial prefix but, whilst there may have been some measure of official planning in its layout, the emperor's name did not lead to anything more than a town of modest size and importance.

William Stukeley, the 18th-century antiquarian, produced a plan of Chelmsford in around 1758 showing the traditional playing-card shape of larger Roman towns and cities and erroneously and imaginatively placing it on the Chelmsford side of the river instead of in the

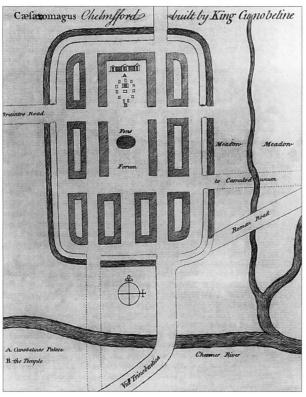

5 William Stukeley's map of Caesaromagus, *c.*1758, which placed the Roman settlement on the wrong side of the River Can.

Moulsham area. Although he had correctly identified Chelmsford/Moulsham as the site of Caesaromagus, it was not until 1840 that John Adey Repton recognised the significance of Roman finds from Moulsham. In 1849 Frederic Chancellor excavated in the Roman Road area and concluded that,

> If, therefore, we could once more produce a photograph of Chelmsford as it appeared from 1,400 to 1,800 years ago, we should see the nucleus of a town with probably some dwellings of a superior character, perhaps a temple, possibly baths and some other public buildings, with numerous other buildings more or less substantial, some no doubt of a quasi-military character. The rivers, instead of being allowed to meander over rich pasture lands, would be confined within proper limits. Certain areas of forest-land would be reclaimed and subject to cultivation, and the old warpaths would be replaced by solid and substantial roadways. The inhabitants still engaged

to some extent in the performance of military duties, but many engaged in manufactures and other peaceful occupations.

Chancellor's assumptions were largely correct. The fort at Caesaromagus was of trapezoidal shape and may have reflected the land boundaries of fields cultivated regularly, though not necessarily continuously, from the Neolithic period up to the development of the Roman town. This cultivation has been evidenced by the discovery of a buried soil and small, abraded, mostly flint-tempered pottery found generally distributed over excavated sites in the town. The fort, in lower Moulsham, was of timber construction and, with others at Great Chesterford and Kelvedon, suggests effective garrisoning of the area. A smaller enclosure to the south of the fort may have been for cavalry troops. Baths and a religious area were also set up outside its precincts. The baths were altered towards the end of the first century and a circular *laconicum*, a sort of sauna, was constructed. The military enclosure was surrounded by a wooden palisade at first but later an earth rampart and ditch were made. Archaeologists have concluded that the enclosure was a 'road station' or staging point for travellers, notably

6 Sketch of the bath building discovered in 1849-50 by Frederic Chancellor in the Roman Road area of Moulsham. The columns of tiles supported the floor and allowed warm air to circulate beneath it. Walls then stood to a height of approximately one metre.

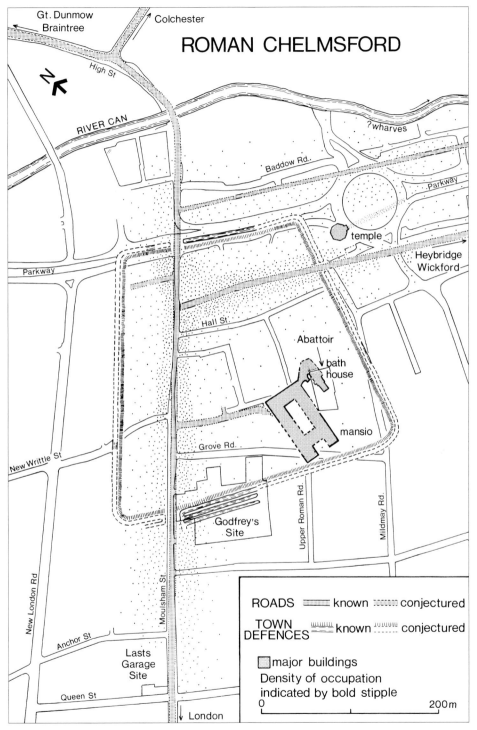

7 Caesaromagus in the early second century. The stippling indicates that the majority of residents lived and probably worked on the sides of the main road. A site on the north side of Hall Street bore indications of horn-core workings.

8   Reconstruction of the *mansio* from an original watercolour by Frank Gardiner. An impressive masonry building with attached bath building combined administrative, postal and accommodation facilities.

government officials who could change horses and rest before continuing their journeys. The enclosure was divided in the second century into building plots.

The principal roads in Roman Britain were laid down for military purposes and improved to serve the *Cursus Publicus*, once described as the Department of Transport and the Royal Mail rolled into one. Incidentally, it is possible that Caesaromagus was accessible by water from

Heybridge during the Roman period. From about A.D. 120 the earlier 'road station' was replaced by a *mansio*, according to Pliny a station, halting place or night quarters, one of many *mansiones* in the Antonine Itinerary. The Itinerary, of early third-century date, gave a list for the whole of Europe of the principal routes used by Roman officials and described where they could confidently expect courier gigs, wagons or coaches to be available. Local

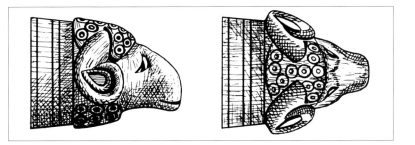

9 A hollow cast copper alloy ram's head, partly filled with lead. This may have been the terminal to a patera handle, a round flat dish used for sacrificial libations, or it could be a furniture fitting.

10 The head of a Medusa, one of the three Gorgons, with snakes for hair, made in jet and part of a hoard of jet objects. She is of the 'beautiful-pathetic' type and is one of very few found in Roman Britain.

11 Reconstruction of a jet necklace, probably made of Whitby jet, like the Medusa's head, at a workshop in York in the middle of the fourth century. It may be from the personal effects of a wealthy lady.

12 Lion's head spout from a mortarium of the second century, made in terra sigillata or samian, a fine, hard, burnished red ware. A mortarium had a rough inner surface for pounding or rubbing vegetables. Any liquid produced could be poured through the lion's mouth.

13 Samian ware was usually stamped with the maker's name. In this case ALBUCIUS was the maker.

14 Base silver denarius of the Roman emperor Septimius Severus, reigned A.D. 193-211. He came to Britain in 208 and, amongst other things, repaired Hadrian's Wall. He died at York aged 65 years.

15 Gold solidus of the Emperor Constantine III, reigned A.D. 407-11. He was proclaimed emperor by the legions in Britain but was captured by a general of Honorius, A.D. 393-423 and executed. Found at Good Easter with solidi of Honorius and Arcadius, A.D. 383-408, the reverse shows Constantine holding a standard, with his foot on a captive. It was made at Triers, Germany. (Photograph: Paul Starr)

16 Bone pin with spherical head, *c.*A.D. 200 to late fourth century. Such pins were often used by ladies to dress their hair.

communities were required to maintain roads and provide horses and their feed as well as ensure the upkeep of installations and their fittings and the vehicles used on the roads. It is known that the *Cursus Publicus* was revamped by Hadrian (reigned A.D. 117-138), which fits with the date of Chelmsford's *mansio*.

Caesaromagus' possession of such an establishment added to its importance in the area. The complex, comprising a rectangular building surrounding a large courtyard on all sides, was first built in timber and shortly afterwards in masonry. The military baths and *laconicum* were incorporated into the extensive and largely self-sufficient block, which is likely to have had an additional administrative function, and was joined to the main road by a new street. The complex probably contained a number of suites with a modest level of finish consistent with the housing of travellers of relatively high standing. Floors were tessellated and the plastered walls painted in plain colours. There were also some larger rooms and it is clear that substantial numbers of people could be accommodated in separate groups. In the mid-to late second century substantial alterations were made to the bath buildings. The *laconicum* was demolished *c.*250 but repairs and alterations to the cold plunge over a long period suggest

that the *mansio* was still in use until the end of the Roman period.

From the beginning of the second century there was also rapid development of long, narrow strip-houses and commercial premises. These were built along the main road in timber and wattle and daub with two or three rooms and a corridor down one side. These thatched buildings would normally have had gravel or clay floors, though occasionally they were planked. Commercial ones would have opened at the front on to the street. Caesaromagus became a market centre where the countryside produce of local people could be exchanged for goods or services. Archaeological finds have shown that there was iron-smithing and pottery production and it is probable that imported goods, too, would have been available. Copper alloy objects were made, as were bone pins and other bone objects and worked animal horn.

Whilst the south of Britain was largely peaceful in the Roman period, there were occasional major disturbances in other parts of the country which impinged upon the town. There may have been a revolt in Wales in 169, and it is known that in 175 Britain's troops were reinforced by 5,500 Sarmatian cavalry. Later in the century the governor of Britain, Clodius Albinus, a man of noble birth and good reputation, claimed the succession to the empire but was subsequently defeated near Lyons in France in 197 and he killed himself. For whatever reason, between 160 and 175 considerable earthen defences were erected to protect the *mansio*. Other Essex towns were similarly fortified at about this time. In Caesaromagus some domestic buildings were destroyed in the process, and it was not until the early third century that the southern part of the defences was flattened to allow the building of new structures.

The religious site associated with the early fort may originally have been a sacred grove with a votive post and pit where visitors could deposit brooches, finger rings, pins, coins and even a complete bracelet. The bones of many sheep have been found in the area, presumably the remains of sacrificial animals. A religious building erected on the site in the first century comprised two separate spaces, one with an apse. Whilst there is evidence of building and re-building on the plot, which was to the east of the fort and approximately under the modern Odeon roundabout, it was not until the early fourth century that an identifiable temple was erected to an octagonal design. Termed Romano-Celtic, the temple was not unsophisticated, containing as it did a *cella* or shrine and an ambulatory or walking area similar to a cloister. It was made in flint, tile and stucco and had a floor area of some 232 square metres.

It may have been dedicated to Mercury, the messenger of the gods, reverenced as the patron of artists, orators, travellers, merchants and, curiously, thieves. Another temple to the south of the *mansio* is possible, and a ritual horse burial has been identified elsewhere in the town.

The Christian practice of burying the dead within the community close to the place of worship, in a churchyard, was not followed by the Romans who, by law, were required to cremate or bury their loved ones outside the town precincts, usually alongside roads. Caesaromagus' burial place was on the London-Colchester road to the south of the town, hence the discovery of buried remains in the area of Rothesay Avenue, for example, and at Godfrey's Mews, where two burials lay within a mausoleum, one in a stone coffin, just outside the town gates.

In 410 the emperor Honorius, who had remained helplessly at Ravenna whilst Rome was sacked in August of that year – just one aspect of the collapse of the western division of the Roman Empire – wrote to the citizens of Britain telling them to undertake their own defence. This was not a withdrawal of legions – they had long gone to Italy or Gaul – but a reply to a request for help. Caesaromagus, having already declined from its peak population in the second century, further declined in the fourth and early fifth centuries, long distance trade having been cut off by the devastation of Gaul by Vandals and others. Rome had administered Britain for over 350 years, a period equal to the distance in time between the present day and the early Stuarts, but once the authority of the empire was gone the *mansio* had little purpose and the town was gradually abandoned and its buildings fell prey to stone and timber robbers. Since there is evidence of

17 Reconstruction of the Romano-Celtic temple built in the early fourth century and comprising two concentric units in an octagonal form well known in Britain and on the continent. Built of flint, tile and stucco, the temple was for pagan worship.

continuing large-scale agricultural use of surrounding land, it may be assumed that the fine *mansio* found its way into the structures of local farmers and builders.

Raids by Saxon pirates, from the area of Schleswig-Holstein in present-day Germany, had begun in the late second century, particularly in the Wash and the Thames estuary. The Romans had built forts against this menace, at Reculver in Kent in the early third century, for example, and later at Bradwell on Sea. In the last thirty years of the third century the large numbers of coin hoards attest to sustained attacks. It was *c.*430, however, that substantive settlements first grew up as the

result of an invitation by the British under Vortigern – a British rather than Roman title, not a name – to protect the province against other attacks, thereby continuing a practice already in use. In *c.*442 a serious revolt of the Saxons took place which established their authority in the south-east of England. By the late fifth century family groups in large numbers were coming here seeking land to farm, for the Saxons were not town dwellers.

There is virtually no evidence of Saxon occupation in Chelmsford itself, although a short-lived building was erected within the temple. Outside the town there was a settlement at Springfield Lyons within the circular

Bronze-Age earthwork. Its cemetery has hundreds of inhumation and cremation burials, the confirmed hundred of the latter buried in pots. Of the 103 certain inhumations, one third contained grave goods, including knives, spears and shield bosses, finger rings, buckles and domestic utensils, glass and amber beads, and pottery decorated with line and dot and with stamping. The form and fabric of these pots give a date from the mid-fifth century to the late sixth century. In the same area a later Saxon settlement dating from the ninth to 11th centuries contained over a dozen structures, including one large building about twenty metres long by eight metres across which was probably divided internally into smaller sections. The site may have been occupied until the 12th century.

The community, overlooking large parts of the fertile Chelmer valley, would no doubt have continued the age-old hunting and gathering but crops would also have been cultivated and livestock managed. Evidence suggests it would have been moderately prosperous. Certainly there were riches in the area. In the late 19th century, men digging for gravel behind Clobbs Row in Broomfield discovered a princely burial, which included a sword decorated with gold studs set with precious stones, a bronze pan containing two glasses and two turned wooden cups with rims of gilt bronze. In the bottom of the grave were two wooden buckets and a two-gallon iron cauldron. Such was the importance of the finds that they were deposited at the British Museum and, incidentally, illustrated in the *Victoria County History* of 1903 in colour!

The invasion of the Angles, Jutes and Saxons gradually culminated in the merging of the indigenous population and its Romano-British background with the invaders' German traditions. There was no town at Chelmsford and its site might be best described as merely a quarry for building materials. The Norman Conquest brought new land owners/developers who would begin to build in this virtually empty space and establish the shape of the town that can still be seen today.

Two

A New Beginning

Within this manor ... is scituate the towne of Chelmsforde ... well scituated with moe than three hundred habitacions, divers of them seemelye for gentlemen ...

From the commentary to the Walker map 1591

The Roman settlement of Caesaromagus was gone and the settlement at Chelmsford shifted after 1066 from Moulsham to the other side of the river Can. Geographically, the central position of Chelmsford/Moulsham between London and Colchester assured the revival of a community here. Its name came not from the river now called the Chelmer but, supposedly, from a Saxon migrant called Ceolmaer. The crossing place of the Can became known as Ceolmaer's ford, later Celmeresford, variously

18 Cartoon of Bishop Maurice from *The Story of Chelmsford*, published in 1948 by R.J. Thompson, son of the late proprietor of the *Essex Chronicle*, for 6d. This was a light-hearted survey of the town's history.

spelt even in the 17th century and later. Moulsham also took its name from a Saxon, the area becoming Muls Ham, the home farm of Mul.

At the time of Domesday Book, the manor of Chelmsford was simply a small rural farm containing only four households. Moulsham had 12 households. Both manors were held by the Church, the former by the Bishop of London, in whose diocese Essex stood, who also held Middlesex and part of Hertfordshire, and the latter by the Abbot of Westminster. Domesday Book of 1086 noted that 'Celmeresfort was held by Bishop William in the time of King Edward and is now held by the Bishop [of London] ...Wood for three hundred swine. Thirty acres of meadow...it is worth eight pounds'. 'Moulsham has always been held by St Peter [i.e. Westminster Abbey], ... wood for four hundred swine. Thirty acres of meadow ... it was worth nine pounds, now twelve'. Traffic bypassed the area and travellers between London and Colchester took their route through Writtle, a royal manor of 194 households, to avoid the perennial flooding of the Can and the Chelmer. In the six hundred years since the Romans left their bridges would have collapsed, and it was not until Bishop

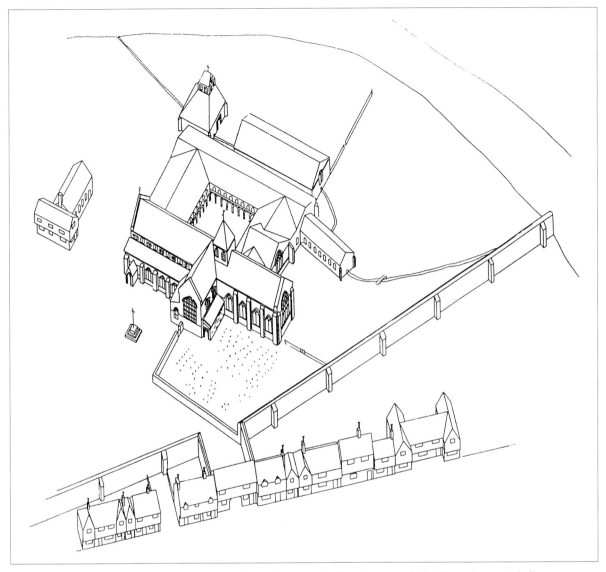

19 Reconstruction of the Dominican Friary by Andrew Harris, showing part of Moulsham Street, including the gateway. A man-made watercourse from the River Can serves the single-storey building. The building at the north-west corner is the kitchen, later to house the first grammar school in the town.

Maurice built new bridges in about 1100 that the town's pivotal position in the county was restored.

Whilst the new bridge restored the main route, the second crucial innovation came in 1199, when Bishop William de St Mere Eglise, Bishop of London, was granted a charter by King John to hold a market. In the following year, a further charter allowed Bishop William to allot freehold plots in the market area, and in 1201 he was granted the right to hold an annual fair on 1 May and the three following days. King John himself came to Chelmsford on 21 March of that year on a journey from York to London. The charters enabled William to establish not only a town but also a means

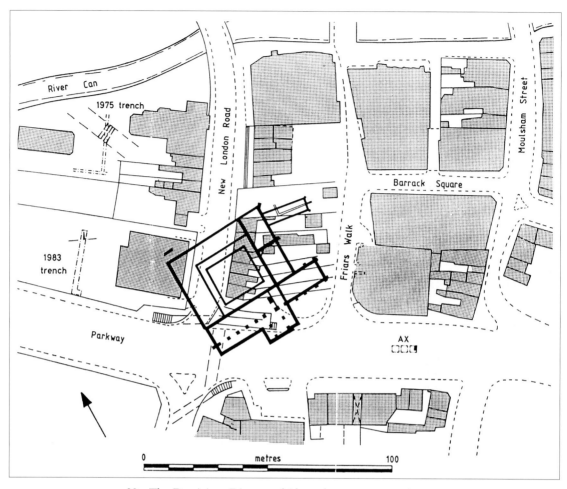

20 The Dominican Friary overlaid on the current street layout.

for making money, 'for the profit and better-ment of our church and our successors'. Those who came to take up the freeholds in the new market were making an investment and all were from outside the immediate area, including some from France, one of whom was known as Henry the Norman. These freehold plots could be conveyed, they were subject to annual manorial rents, and they required an oath of fealty to the bishop as lord and attendance at his court. Freeholders became known as towns-men or burgesses. Moulsham did not have the same rights and that may account for its being Chelmsford's poor relation.

The area of the new town, for that was what was being created, stood away from the bishop's manor house, Bishop's Hall, which was sited to the north of what was to become Chelmsford near the modern junction of Rec-tory Lane and New Street, under the former premises of Messrs Hoffmann's, now Anglia Polytechnic University. The town was to be based round a triangular market place, the junction of a road running south to Bishop Maurice's bridge with an offshoot leading east towards Colchester, north to Bishop's Hall and north-west to Writtle and Braintree, now called High Street, Springfield Road, New Street and

21 Jill Macaulay, Excavation Assistant and later Assistant Curator at Chelmsford Museum, with a complete medieval earthenware jug found in the culvert to the bottom right of the picture. The culvert led water into the reredorter (privy) channel to remove waste. The reredorter dated from *c.*1300 onwards.

Duke Street respectively. A church dedicated to St Mary was built in the early 13th century which dominated the upper end of the axial north-south High Street.

Bishop William's initiative clearly provided dividends. By the middle of the 13th century, Chelmsford was the county town of Essex, for here the King's itinerant Justices began to meet on a regular basis, establishing an Assize, a function discharged until 1971 when the County Court system was introduced. In 1218 a writ instructed the Justices to gather at Chelmsford, the only place in Essex to be so named. From that time Chelmsford was the usual meeting place and it attracted a great number of people having legal or county business to transact, although the town itself was still physically small. Its future growth was the result of its central geographical position and of the trades and professions drawn here to service the needs of incoming and passing travellers. The two functions of market and county town provided the impetus for future development.

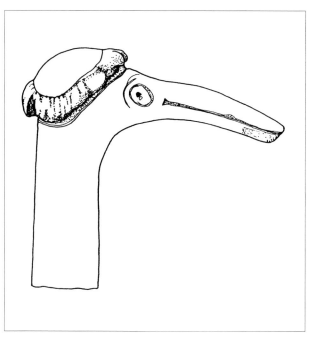

22   The lower part of an antler probably used as a riding crop. Both sides are similarly carved to give the impression of a bird with the crown having the appearance of a priest's tonsure.

The shape of the market area was triangular, bounded by the church at one end and by plots, some over 600 feet long, on either side of the street and sloping down towards the river, with a central channel in the middle of the road. Because of the bend of the Chelmer before it joined the Can, plots were shorter towards the bridge than at the church end of the High Street. By 1400 many different and individual buildings made up the High Street, with differing roof pitches, most of the roofs being thatched though some may have been tiled. By this time there would have been few gaps left in the street to infill.

On the south side of the churchyard stood a 'house' and, below it, an open-sided structure called 'Le Tolhouse', used for sessions of the Assize and the Justices. The open building was also used by farmers as a corn market, becoming known as the 'Cornemarket' or 'Markett Cross'.

23   Friary gateway by W. Brown. The gateway survived until its demolition in 1857.

24   Moulsham Bridge or the Great Bridge, as shown in the badge of Moulsham High School. The bridge and the two rivers are also seen in both versions of the town's armorial bearings – those of the original borough and of the borough enhanced by the inclusion of the Rural District Council after 1974.

Plots had also been disposed of in the High Street itself, at first for stallholders to set up their trading points. Gradually structures were erected, creating a sort of island of buildings. The area became known as Middle Row or Shoprow. South of the Shoprow were the fish market and the leather market and further down were poultry sellers and butchers.

A public water supply came from Burgeyswell (later Burgess Well), which rose at the back of the present Civic Centre, was channelled through elm pipes across, to and under Duke Street to emerge by the Cross. It then flowed down the High Street, turning left into Springfield Road (known also as Springfield Lane or Colchester Lane), and into the Gullet which ran between the Chelmer and the Can. This constant supply of spring water was used as a means of cleansing the street and the market traders threw rubbish into it. With other waste being tipped directly into the two rivers, they were often in a foul condition. Pigs were let loose to clear rubbish remaining in the street but the cure became worse than the disease and by-laws were enacted to control this menace.

Market days each Friday supplied innkeepers with, for example, corn, fish, poultry and other meats, plus ale and wine. Other traders supplied clothes and shoes, and provision for horses had been available for some time in the form of saddlery and the services of farriers and blacksmiths. In 1494 Chelmsford was designated by Act of Parliament the town in Essex to house the standard weights and measures from which copies were made, stamped with an H, to be inspected twice each year under the jurisdiction of the bailiff and Justices. There was uniformity, too, of standard, for example 14 pounds making a stone and 26 stone a sack of wool.

The town grew under the hand of powerful ecclesiastics, and the influence of the Church was to be felt even more on the establishment in Moulsham of a friary. The foundation was sited on the north side of Parkway at its junction with New London Road. The Dominicans or Black Friars' house was founded in the mid–13th century, though the exact date is not known. It was not solitary or contemplative but preached to the populace, took care of the sick and taught the poor. The order enjoyed both local and royal support. The brothers met Edward III, for example, when he visited Chelmsford in 1342 and he gave them alms of 3s. 4d. Their church was of some pretension, with even the culvert bringing water from the Burgess Well to the site being faced in Caen stone and floored with Purbeck marble. The fresh water was used not only for culinary and washing purposes but for the disposal of waste matter into the river.

The rebuilding of two of the town's important landmarks came within a period of fifty years, the first in the late 14th century and the second in the middle of the 15th century, work continuing into the 16th century. The bridge built in 1100 was in a poor state by the 1370s and, although manor court records attribute its rebuilding to the Bishop of London, Simon Sudbury, it was the Abbot of Westminster who commissioned Henry Yevele, the king's master mason, to rebuild the structure in 1372 at the cost of £73 6s. 8d. Of three arches, the bridge was erected in stone and was to serve the increasing traffic on the main road until it was replaced by the present bridge at the end of the 18th century. The exact date sequence of the rebuilding of the parish church is not known, but it is clear that the modest building of the early 15th century was deemed to be inappropriate to the

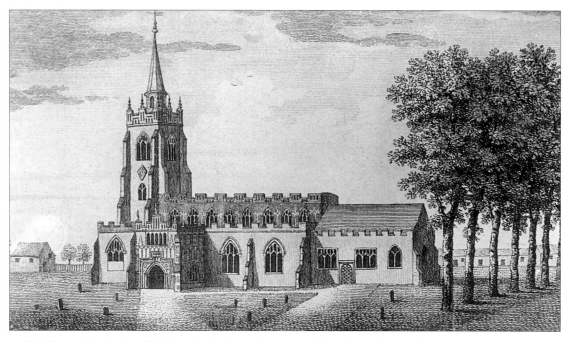

25 The parish church of St Mary in the late 18th century, before the collapse of the nave in 1800 destroyed part of the medieval building.

pretensions of the county town. The rebuilding in Perpendicular style added a new feature, a bell tower, in the late 15th century although other parts of the structure had been begun in the 1420s. Locally occurring flint rubble mixed with stone blocks was used to create a chancel, north and south chapels, nave with clerestory, north and south aisles, porch and tower. The tower and porch remain but much of the rest of the church had to be rebuilt in the early 19th century.

Town affairs were managed by the bishop's steward and bailiff, the latter living in the town, the former making occasional visits to conduct the manor court. The bailiff collected rents and tolls and was responsible for the promulgation of the orders of the steward and the court. Men had, however, responsibility for their own actions. Long before this period, the law of the land demanded that all men be associated in groups of ten or twelve responsible for each other's good behaviour. There were many exceptions, such as lords (lay or spiritual) and members of their households. Men who held freehold land were exempt for their land was their pledge. All others over the age of 12 were bound by a tithing of frankpledge, under a chief pledge. In the reign of Henry I a legal writer stressed: 'It is lawful for every lord to summon his man to right in his court.' Twice each year the sheriff visited the court of each hundred or wapentake to 'view the frankpledge' or manor court leet. The king often granted an individual lord the right to hold the view of frankpledge and such a grant had been made to the Bishop of London in 1199. It was the bishop's court, therefore, which superintended the tithings, punished wrongdoers and protected the public from dishonest tradesmen who, for example, broke the weight requirements on bread. Similarly, the Abbot of Westminster had Henry III's grant and, like the Bishop, he had his own gallows, pillory and whipping post.

As the magnates of England had responsibilities towards the king (William I, for example, relied on barons and church leaders to provide him with 4,000 knights), so the chief pledges were obliged to attend court leet to report on local matters of mis-behaviour. Numbers of chief pledges varied, but just over thirty was the average. These were leading townsmen who held office for life or until they left the town. They in turn chose tithings members to inspect meat, ale and other commodities. They also selected the constables from amongst the ranks of the chief pledges, of whom two were confirmed in their annual appointment by the bishop, and affeerers, where again two of the four were confirmed. These men were appointed to assess the levels of fine on wrongdoers. Not only were there matters of dishonesty but also of violence. There were murders and assaults, sometimes even on the constables, as when William Fayrer had his 'head broken' in 1468.

Not that the leaders of the town were at all times entirely honest and worthy. In 1380, when Richard II's parliament enacted a third poll tax within three years, requiring three groats (three fourpenny pieces) from all people over the age of 15 except for beggars, there was connivance in fraud by the constables and chief pledges in Chelmsford. As Hilda Grieve said: 'So here you have a remarkable example of the governors of the town and all the towns-men themselves, all of one mind, uniting in one colossal fraud.' In both Moulsham and Chelmsford, the numbers liable for the tax, according to local lists, had halved since 1377.

When commissioners were sent to check the returns Essex and Kent revolted, followed by 28 other counties across the country. King's and sheriff's exchequer writs and manor rolls were seized by the rebels and many of them were publicly burned in Chelmsford. Kentish rebels under Wat Tyler moved on London as did Essex men. At Mile End the boy king, Richard II, offered clemency, later repudiated by himself and his Parliament. Amongst the casualties of the so-called Peasants' Revolt was Tyler himself and the Archbishop of Canterbury, Simon Sudbury, once Lord of Chelmsford as Bishop of London, who was dragged from the Tower chapel and murdered on Tower Hill, his head being set on London Bridge.

The King subsequently entered Essex and, from 1 to 6 July, resided at Chelmsford with his ministers and secretariat, overseeing the process of pacification as well as presiding over the seat of government of all England for a week. At Le Tolhouse the new Chief Justice, Sir Robert Tresilian, who replaced the murdered former holder of the post, dealt with many of the rebels. At least a dozen were hanged at Gallows Field, now the site of Primrose Hill at Rainsford.

By the end of the 15th century Chelmsford was a confirmed economic success and plots in the High Street were difficult to obtain. Some Londoners moved in, perhaps as an investment, and other plots were owned by religious foundations who used the income to pay chaplains to say masses at the parish church as well as private prayers for individuals. By the mid-16th century, there may have been about a thousand people living in the town. One of the newcomers was Thomas Mildmay, a mercer, a dealer in textile fabrics and especially costly materials, who came to the town in

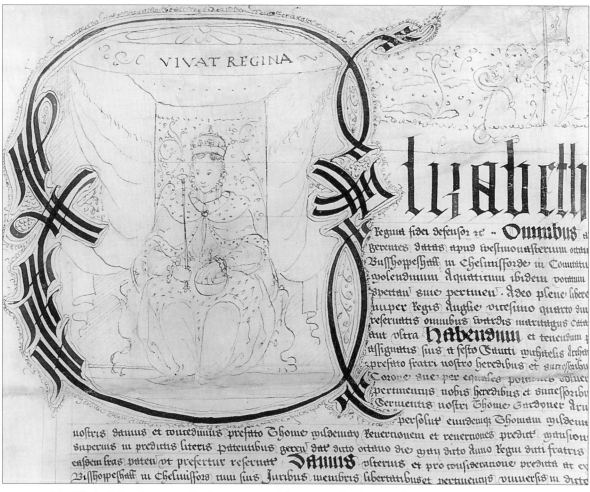

26 Elizabeth I as shown on the Crown grant of the manor of Bishop's Hall to Thomas Mildmay, 24 July 1563, five years after her accession to the throne.

1506 and set up his stall. Within twenty years he was a wealthy man.

Although three of his five sons followed their father's trade, his heir, also Thomas, did not and instead entered government service. He was appointed in 1535 as one of the commissioners surveying and valuing the property of the Church for Henry VIII. Termed an auditor of the Court of Augmentations, which later dealt with confiscated properties, he toured eastern England with his colleagues prior to the confiscation. The Dissolution of

the Monasteries duly came in 1538. In 1540, he purchased the manor of Moulsham, which included the Black Friars seized in 1538, for £622 5s. 8d., where two years later he began to build a grand house. He and his brother also benefited from the subsequent dissolution of chantries in 1547, endowments to clerics derived from property, in the reign of Edward VI, purchasing the property of the Guild of St John, mostly in Moulsham.

In 1557 he was Sheriff of Essex but was still not master of the manor of Chelmsford, which was the property successively of Henry VIII, Edward VI, Queen Mary and Queen Elizabeth. In July 1563 he acquired the manor of Bishop's Hall, Chelmsford, for £1,202 2s. 9d., which included the market, the Tolhouse and the Cross of Chelmsford. This was a huge sum considering that even a hundred years later, according to a broadsheet of 1651, a master mason received £4 per year plus 10 shillings 'livery', an allowance for food and clothes, a plumber £3 5s. plus 10 shillings 'livery', a weaver £3 plus 10 shillings 'livery', a best woman servant 50 shillings and a chamber-maid 30 shillings. Thomas now owned both Moulsham and Chelmsford, thus uniting them for the first time.

Perhaps it was the delay in acquiring what he must have coveted which made Thomas Mildmay entail his estate to his eldest son and his male heirs, reverting to the male heirs of his other sons if the male line of his heir, also Thomas, failed. This legal device succeeded in keeping the estates intact until the middle of the 19th century. Thomas the auditor died in 1566 and was succeeded by Sir Thomas Mildmay, who married in 1580 into the barony of the Fitzwalters. He took a great interest in local affairs, including the provision of troops against the expected Spanish invasion in 1588.

Whilst Mildmay's manor court was more efficient by the end of the 16th century, the Justices were taking on wider jurisdiction with regard to breaches of the peace. The parish, too, under Tudor legislation, was taking on the responsibility for the poor and for highways, with parish officers, overseers and surveyors assuming civil functions for which they had to raise funds by rate, supervised by the Justices. The Statute of 1598 declared:

> Be it enacted … that the churchwardens of every parish and four substantial householders there …
> who shall be nominated yearly in Easter Week, under the hand and seal of two or more Justices of the Peace in the same county … shall be called Overseers of the Poor of the same parishes.

Magistrates also regulated both the rate of wages, from 1591/2, and the licensing of keepers of ale-houses under an act of 1552. The manor court, however, retained the resolution of problems relating to the bylaws and to conflicts between neighbours and between landlords and their tenants. Both Moulsham and Chelmsford had parish officers and this emphasised the separation of town and hamlet which was not to be fully concluded until the incorporation of the two in a new borough in 1888.

As always, there were the poor, who had to be found accommodation and also work unless they were incapable through illness. The parish register of 1557 records: 'Here were eleven pore women buryed that lived in the strete'. In 1541, however, many of the trades and degrees of the townspeople are mentioned: 'bocher, carryer, cobeler, cutteler, draper, buckle maker, breuer, fletcher, labourer, mercer, esquire, gentyleman, osteler, tapster and colermaker'.

The late 16th century saw the gradual change from temporary stalls to permanent structures in Middle Row, although the first building was not set up until the 1630s. This led to the *de facto* creation of Back Street (parallel with Fore Street or High Street), also known as Conduit Street and later Tindal Street. It added congestion to an already busy town. In 1591 the parish church was said to be able to house 'two thousand people or more'. The extent of the town and its features can be seen in the map of 1591 and its accompanying volume, produced for Sir Thomas by his steward, John Latham, surveyor, Edward Moryson, and

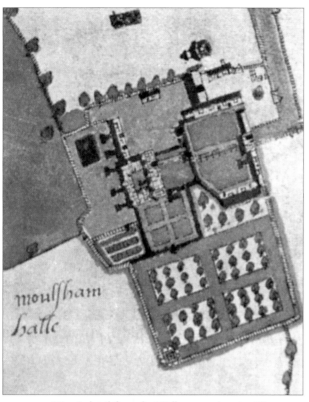

27 A detail from the Walker map showing Thomas Mildmay's residence at Moulsham Hall. Like the main part of the map, buildings are laid down to show windows, doors and chimneys.

'architector', John Walker, who gave his name to the splendid map, 'A Trew Platt of the Manor'. The volume states that: 'Chelmersforde is one goodlye manor situate in the harte of the countye of Essex in good and holesome aire, convenientelie and well housed and well builte for timber and tile ...'. It has 'manie fayre innes' and is 'a greate thorowefare and markett towne weekely uppon the Friday, in which markett are to be sold an abundance of victualles and wares ...'.

In 1594 the mapmaker John Norden said of Essex: 'This shire is moste fatt, frutefull, and full of profitable thinges, exceding (as farr as I can finde) anie other shire, for the generall comodeties, and the plentie.' Of 'Chelmersforde corrupté Chensforde', he echoes Walker and

adds: 'It is well watered and standeth in a frutfull soyle. A thorowfare of greate receyte and good enterteynement muche frequented.'

This last remark may be a reference to bull-baiting, archery or just a 'fayre inne', but he may have been remembering Chelmsford's reputation for staging some of the most elaborate plays, mostly of a religious nature, in the county. The last play in the town appears to have been in 1576, the same year the churchwardens finally sold off the costumes and scenery built up over some years which had been loaned to other towns and villages for their plays. Among items supplied to Heybridge, for example, for one of their performances were: a coat of leather for Christ; a temple, a hell, sheep's hooks, whips, prophets' caps, flags for the devil, clouds and giants. The plays were stopped because they were a financial loss.

Walker's map shows, on the south-west side of the Can, a single building set back from the ones lining Moulsham Street. It has the words 'fryers' and 'fre schoole howse' next to it and represents, except for the Friary gateway which was demolished in 1857, all that remained of the disbanded and demolished religious foundation. It was in this building, the friars' former refectory, later drawn by William Stukeley, that a free grammar school was established in 1551. There had been schools before, at the end of the 14th and in the early 16th centuries; now came a properly established place of learning with two of its four governors being Thomas Mildmay, the auditor, and his brother Sir Walter Mildmay, a general surveyor of the Court of Augmentations. To give status to the new school, which still thrives four hundred and fifty years later, Thomas sent his son, also Thomas, to be one of the pupils. The school remained at the 'fryers' until 1627, a move becoming necessary

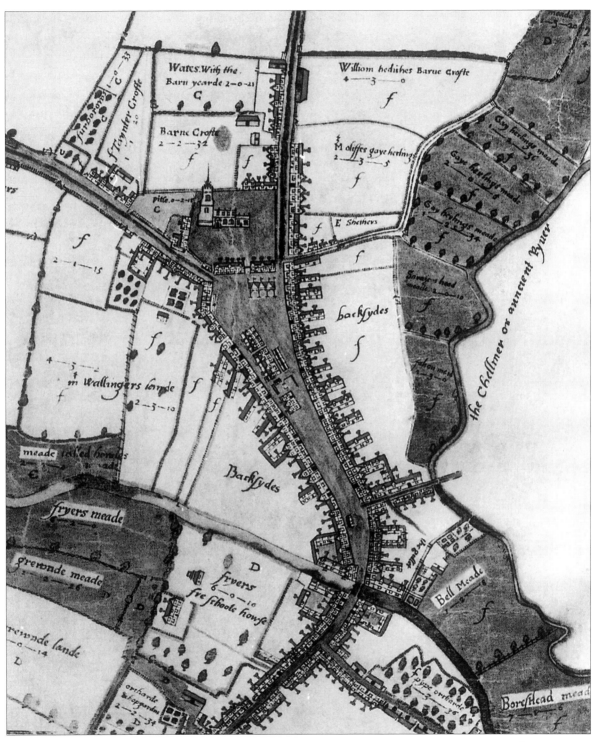

28 The Walker map of 1591, produced for Sir Thomas Mildmay, 'A Trew Platt of the Manor'. The map shows the shape of the town we still know today. Familiar names include Bell Meade and Sarazen's head meade.

29 Reconstruction of Chelmsford market place, based upon the Walker map, from an original oil painting by Roger Massey-Ryan. The establishment of Middle Row is clear, as are the Sessions House and the parish church. New Street runs to Bishop's Hall and Duke Street into the countryside.

30 A shilling piece issued 1551-3, with the mint-mark tun of Edward VI who reigned from 1547-53.

31 The Grammar School in the late 18th century was housed in the buildings erected or converted in 1627. In the background can be seen the spire of the parish church.

then after the roof was said to have fallen in, fortunately when master and students were out. A site in Duke Street, or Brochole Street, approximately on the site of the modern County Hall, was selected and a two-storey school house erected. Part of the *George Inn*, also known as the Chequers or Springfields, was converted for the use of the school master. Much of the cost of the work was defrayed by Lord Petre of Ingatestone. The school was to remain here until 1891, when it removed to its present site in Broomfield Road.

As the King Edward VI Grammar School was being established as a seat of learning and progress, two barbaric practices were still being carried out in Chelmsford. In 1555 Thomas Wats of Billericay was publicly burned in the town for failing to say mass and for holding secret and/or unlawful religious meetings. In

1582, after his arrest the previous year, John Payne, a Catholic priest trained at the English College at Douai, was executed at Chelmsford for treason. Having spent eight months at the Tower of London, where he was 'most violently tormented on the rack', he forgave George Eliot, his accuser and an apostate Catholic: 'I forgive his monstrous wickedness and defy his malicious inventions.' On the scaffold he said, 'I confess that I die a Christian Catholic priest'. In a *Briefe History* of 1582, Cardinal Allen said, 'They very courteously caused men to hang on his feet and set the knot to his ear and suffered him to hang to death,' to avoid the agony of quartering. His name is perpetuated at St John Payne School, Chelmsford's Roman Catholic secondary school.

These examples of religious homicide run alongside the hounding and execution of witches. The rigours of legal prosecution for witches arose in the second half of the 16th century and the first three-quarters of the seventeenth. Because the Protestants disapproved of the Roman Catholic rite of exorcism, which in the past had controlled those 'possessed of the devil', a legal remedy was substituted. Often 'witches' were accused by those who had in some way cheated or treated them ungenerously. The accused were often eccentric or of a disagreeable appearance. Certainly there was a general belief in witchcraft, even among the educated. In 1624, for example, John Crushe was ordered to apologise to the minister and churchwardens of Hawkwell, Rochford for burning 'a lamb which, he sayeth, was bewitched'. He performed this task on the common 'and soe set fire to the Common (being full of rubbish) burneing a great compasse … affrighting also the country round about'.

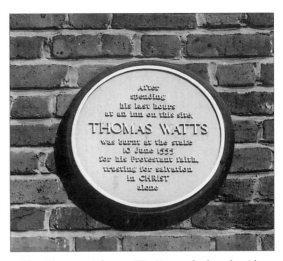

32 Plaque to Thomas Wat(t)s attached to the side wall of a shop facing on to the High Street, near the Stone Bridge.

Between 1560 and 1599, 163 witches were prosecuted at Chelmsford and those who were convicted were hanged there. A pamphlet published after the trial and hanging of 'three notorious witches' in 1589 offered to disclose 'the divelish practises and keeping of their spirits whose fourmes are heerein truelye proportioned'. Unfortunately, the harassment of so-called witches continued into the following century, most notably in 1645, when the activities of the self-styled Witchfinder General, Matthew Hopkins, principally in the north of the county round Mistley, led to the hanging of 19 'witches' in Chelmsford. Hopkins, who was paid to search out these unfortunate women, employed torture to extort his 'confessions'. In 1611 a Chelmsford house of correction was established in Wymonds, a timber-framed building opposite Springfield Lane (Road), to imprison those convicted of relatively minor offences from all over the county. The waste problem in the town worsened until in 1631 four farmers were appointed by the manor court to collect rubbish, including dung, every three weeks. The execution of witches

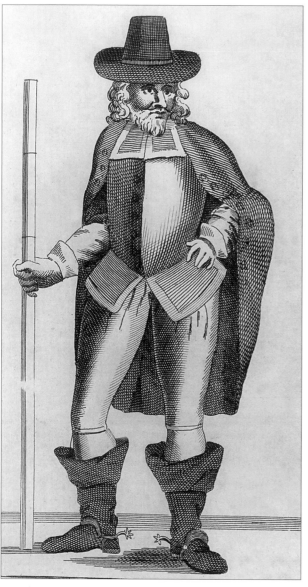

33 Matthew Hopkins, the Witchfinder General, who inspired terror in East Anglia with his investigations into witchcraft. Many of his victims were executed in Chelmsford.

a firearm about 3½ feet long), and five musketeers, all pressed men, marched through the town to Chester for service in Ireland, and in 1624 when 750 men left Chelmsford for Dover *en route* to the Palatinate.

Lists of working-class males between the ages of 16 and 60 were compiled by manorial stewards showing those who might be impressed for military service. Constables had the duty to make returns yearly or half-yearly of the fittest to bear arms if needed. Essex had traditionally been required to provide 4,000 foot and 250 horse made up of 20 companies of 200 men, based on hundreds, divisions of the county with their own courts. Each had a captain and equipment was provided by property owners identified by the county's Lord Lieutenant. On the six occasions the Chelmsford Hundred force, comprising 30 parishes and one hamlet, met in the town between 1608 and 1624, between 184 and 200 men were present. Other hundreds also mustered in Chelmsford on occasion, including Witham, Maldon, The Dengie and Rochford. Nominally, 50 Heavy Horse and 100 each from the Northern Hundreds and the Southern Hundreds Light Horse were to meet, usually at Chelmsford, but they were always short of the required number.

These troops were needed in case of invasion or civil unrest and they had to be supported by reserves of gunpowder, match and bullets, and 'other provision for carriages to be kept ready on all occasions'. Ammunition was principally kept at the Moot Hall at Colchester and at the Vestry at Chelmsford. In 1624 a large consignment worth £100 was delivered to Charles Bigland, churchwarden. The money for these supplies had been raised by a county levy of which the Chelmsford Hundred's contribution was £9. The Militia, or Territorial

and heretics no doubt drew crowds of onlookers. The regular musters of the militia in the town must have stimulated local interest and local trade, too, but for very different reasons. There were also irregular visits, as in 1608 when 15 pikemen, 30 caliver men (a caliver is

34 Moulsham Hall in 1638 when Charles I greeted his mother-in-law Marie de Medici.

Force as it became known in the 20th century, was the only large permanent armed force in the kingdom apart from the king's own guards. It was over the control of the Militia and the reform of the Church of England that Charles I (1625–49), refused to yield to the leaders of Parliament. Indeed, he issued a proclamation in May 1642 forbidding his subjects to obey Parliament's Militia Ordinance which transferred control of the Militia to the hands of lords lieutenant sympathetic to Parliament.

The determination of the King to wage war as he thought fit and pay for it by whatever device he deemed necessary led to the opposition of Parliament. The enforcement of his standards, influenced no doubt by his Catholic wife Henrietta Maria, on the Church led to the distress of many, including those who emigrated to the Americas to avoid the demands of Archbishop of Canterbury, Archbishop Laud. Both the political and the religious ramifications of Charles's policies were felt in Chelmsford.

King Charles visited Moulsham Hall in 1638 to greet his mother-in law, Marie de Medici, and escort her to London. P. de la Serre described the visit:

> Her Majesty left ... on 8 November, to pass the night near the market Town of Chensford [sic] in a mansion belonging to Monsieur de Mildmay, a Chevalier of distinction as much for his individual merit as for the antiquity of his noble family. The Queen arrived there at 4 o'clock in the evening but truly I know not how to describe the new and delightful magnificence with which her entry into this part was accompanied. Imagine that all the country folk, men and women, of the neighbourhood were gathered since the morning in various groups throughout the road whereby Her Majesty was to travel without any order or any sort of discipline except what their zeal had imposed upon them.

The Queen was, in short, received with 'a thousand exclamations of joy'.

The King's insistence that High Church rituals should be followed at a time when there was an upsurge in nonconformist thinking and practice led to sometimes violent interdenominational strife. In November 1641 a mob of extremists smashed windows in the parish church, including the coloured glass in the east window which contained not only images of Christ but the arms of those who had subscribed to the re-building of the church two centuries before.

Difficulties had arisen at the church at the beginning of the century when the rector, William Passfield, attempted to nominate one of the three churchwardens without the consent of the parishioners. He was rusticated to Wethersfield, but a subsequent rector, William Michaelson, appointed by James I (1603-25), tried to do the same. He had already incurred the enmity of Sir Thomas Mildmay, the patron of the living, who died in 1625 and was succeeded by his younger brother, Henry, an ardent officer of the militia.

In 1614 Thomas Williamson left money to pay for a monthly sermon to be given by four different preachers a year. Within a few years this had become a single preacher in the form of Thomas Hooker, who became the Reverend Michaelson's curate and friend. Hooker was a powerful speaker and popular orator who condemned the profligacy and profanity of many locals who not only failed to attend church but who were drunken and rowdy and played unsuitable games on the Sabbath. Hooker came from the Puritan side of the church congregation, thus provoking the dissatisfaction of Bishop Laud, then Bishop of London, who determined that he should go. And go he did by 1630, later settling in America and credited with being a founding father of the state of Connecticut. He died in 1647.

The Reverend Doctor Michaelson conformed to Laud's requirements, although a growing number of parishioners dissented from the 'popish' trappings of the Bishop's rites and refused or delayed the payment of Ship Money, a much resented general tax which had previously applied only to ports for underwriting the cost of naval vessels but was now brought in by the King to boost his finances. The dissent grew, and in 1642 the Rev. Michaelson was taken by the throat in his own church and attempts were made to tear from him the surplice which had come to represent a return to Roman Catholic values.

35 Plaque to Thomas Hooker, placed opposite the side of the Shire Hall in the passage leading into the Cathedral churchyard.

36 Plaque to the Society of Friends mounted on the wall opposite the road leading to the Odeon and British Home Stores car park.

The breach between King and Parliament is well recorded elsewhere. In Essex the Lord Lieutenant, the Earl of Warwick, a supporter of the Parliamentary side, raised militia forces which congregated in Chelmsford. Hundreds of undisciplined soldiers, whipped up by local zealots, took over the rector's home, interrupted his services and insulted him. Prayer books were torn up and trampled underfoot. The Rev. Michaelson finally left the town for Oxford, where the King had his headquarters, thence to Holland, returning in 1646 and living quietly in Writtle. By the mid-1640s, however, the town had settled down with a new minister, Mark Mott, and with parish officers of a more ordinary sort, although still senior men of the community. In 1646 a special parish meeting, albeit a Presbyterian one, decided that meetings concerning 'the severall bussynes of the towne tending to the good and welfare thereof' should be held monthly in their several houses. After the relatively recent acrimony and violence, this seems a remarkably conciliatory statement. But at the same time a committee sat in Chelmsford to raise money and men for the Parliamentary cause.

In June 1648 there was a Royalist gathering in the town of several thousand men, who moved on to Boreham to meet with a contingent from Hertfordshire and then marched to Colchester, where they were besieged for several weeks before surrendering. Less than a year later the King was dead and the monarchy abolished. A parish run on Presbyterian lines, with services as required by the Directory of Public Worship, had been established and the Prayer Book was abandoned. Governance of the town was either by court leet or general court baron and the Quarter Sessions, the last increasing its jurisdiction. The lord of the manors, Sir Henry Mildmay, died in 1654 and left his properties to his seven-year-old grandson, also Henry, who was to die in his youth and leave the inheritance to his brother, Benjamin. It was Benjamin who was to succeed

37 Farthing token of William Huchenson, 1658, featuring a rabbit though he was a hop-grower, who died 1686. At the Assizes in February 1677, he was fined 3s., a substantial sum in those days, for failing to attend church on four consecutive Sundays.

house being established in Baddow Lane by the 1680s. The Society of Friends also met in Baddow Lane and had its own building erected there just after the turn of the 18th century. A third meeting house was to follow when a split in the Presbyterian congregation occurred at the beginning of the new century.

During the period of the Commonwealth, only one official copper coin was struck, a farthing. Because of the serious lack of small denominations, towns and traders took it upon themselves to issue small change, and between 1648 and 1672 very large quantities were minted and distributed. Most were halfpennies or farthings, though there are examples of pennies being produced. Traders in Chelmsford were part of this movement and the town produced 22 tokens by different issuers, some of them minting more than one token, between 1656 and 1669. At least nine of the issuers were grocers, not unsurprisingly since they were the general stores of the day, but there was also a clothier, a baker, a vintner, a locksmith, a brazier and an innkeeper. Henry Cordall, a milliner, was also an overseer of the poor in 1643. When

to the Fitzwalter line in 1670 as the 17th Baron, after a long struggle by the family to be recognised in the title.

By this time the Stuart dynasty was re-established, although nonconformist communities continued, with a Presbyterian meeting

38   Halfpenny token of Jasper Eve 1659, bearing the Fruiterers' Arms though Eve was a clothier.

his will was proved in 1671, he left 'To the poor of Chelmsford and Moulsham £3 and to be distributed to the most needy'. Francis Arwaker, a woollen-draper, was a town surveyor in 1643 and later a constable. Thomas Josseline, a grocer, also thought of the poor in his will. He bequeathed, 'To the poor of Chelmsford forty shillings for Bread to be given to them within 14 days after my death'.

The spelling of Chelmsford was correct on most of the tokens produced, but the following variations have been found: Chelmesford, Chensforde, Chelnsford, Chelnesford, Chehnesford and Chernesford. This may be because of a lack of agreement over the spelling of the name of the county town or it may have been the low level of literacy of the day, particularly when the tokens were minted in another part of the country.

In Moulsham there were four issuers: a glazier, a chandler, a flax dresser and an ironmonger, the last represented on his token by a wheel barrow. Here again there were discrepancies in spelling: MOVSHAM, MOUVLSHEM, MOVSOM and MOVLSHAM. At that time V was substituted for U in coin and token legends. Other tokens were issued at Danbury, Much Baddow, Springfield, Waltham Magney (Great Waltham), Littell Walton (Little Waltham) and Writtle. It was not until 1672 that the Royal Mint began to alleviate the problem of the dearth of small coinage by issuing a royal farthing. In August of that year a proclamation ordered the minting of tokens to cease, and warned that anyone disobeying the order would be 'chastised with exemplary severity'. A further token did appear but that was over one hundred years later.

Three

Consolidation and Enhancement

The Town … ranks among the principal ones in Essex
Count Lorenzo Magalotti

In 1669 Cosmo de Medici, Grand Duke of Tuscany, visited Chelmsford on a tour through England. He was received by Charles II, within a decade of his Restoration, with 'high courtesy and consideration'. The King also arranged pleasure trips for him. In Essex de Medici met General George Monck, Duke of Albemarle, who was largely responsible for the return of the King, at New Hall, Boreham. He stayed at the *Black Boy* in Chelmsford and, while his carriages were being prepared, 'his highness took a walk through the town, which from its

39 Chelmsford from Springfield Hill in 1669, executed by an artist who accompanied Cosmo de Medici, Grand Duke of Tuscany, when he visited the town.

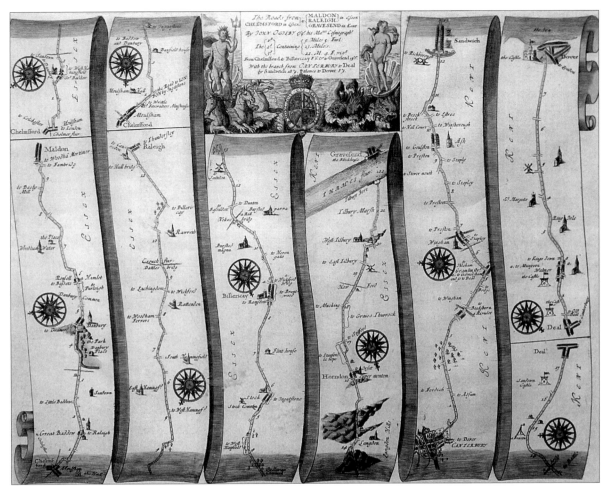

40 A strip map of 1675 by John Ogilby showing the roads from Chelmsford and the distances to be travelled.

population and wealth, ranks among the principal ones in Essex, in the centre of which it stands'. The Duke continued his reign in Tuscany until 1722, a reign described as 'the most unjust and disastrous that Tuscany had ever known'. Nevertheless, his comment on the town can be given some credence. It is known for example that there were, as the commentary to the Walker map had said eighty years before, many fine inns.

In 1662 Parliament introduced the Hearth Tax, a levy of two shillings on every hearth, to make up a shortfall in revenues. This unpopular tax was abolished after 1688. At least 33 per cent of the households of England were exempted from paying the tax on the grounds of poverty. In Moulsham the figure was 64 per cent and in Chelmsford 38 per cent, showing that the latter, though it had its poor, was the wealthier of the two. In 1671 the inns were the largest buildings after Moulsham Hall, which had 22 hearths. The *Cock Inn*, on the present site of Cater House, had 20 as did the *Red Lion* on the west side of the stone bridge, and the *Black Boy*. Eleven others had eight or nine.

The Restoration in due course brought reconciliation. By 1661 Dr Michaelson was back in his rectory and he survived until 1674 to a great age. But the town was to endure one more traumatic event in the 17th century, the onset of bubonic plague in 1665. Essex was badly affected by the infection brought to the county by travellers and tradesmen, who would normally have been welcomed. Colchester was badly hit, almost 5,000 residents, a third of the population, dying. Chelmsford seemed to follow the pattern set by London in 1625 and 1636, with outbreaks in the town earlier in the century in 1625 and 1637.

The first victim in the parish was John Spight, a mat-maker of Moulsham who died at the end of August 1665. The parish overseers, one of whom was Francis Arwaker, a clothier who had issued a token in 1660, normally worked a fortnightly rota relieving the poor in Chelmsford and Moulsham. They decided in the face of such a fearful disease, however, to pay the Moulsham overseer, John Green, £5 to isolate the infection in Moulsham. In addition there were sundry expenses for such services as nursing, grave-digging, nailing up and marking the doors of those affected, and torches and bearers needed to light the burials which took place at night, many of them in the area of the former football club ground near the river. Green successfully prevented the spread of the plague for 34 weeks, the epidemic not reaching Chelmsford until April 1666. At the end of August that year, George Jefferies, a grocer and new churchwarden, recorded that 14 families with 41 members were infected in Chelmsford and 57 families with 122 members in Moulsham, representing six per cent of Chelmsford's households and 35 per cent of Moulsham's. A.F.J. Brown has calculated the population in 1670 to have been 1,725. Hilda Grieve, in her lecture 'The Apprenticeship of a Borough' in 1988, suggested that there cannot have been fewer than 500 victims of the outbreak, representing about a quarter of the population.

The 18th century was to be a period of advancement and visitors were to note Chelmsford's advantages. In 1724 John Macky wrote to a friend abroad: 'Tis a pretty large and populous town, and a great thorowfare from London to the East. The situation of it is charming for it is in a beautiful plain, with a little river running through it. The inns are very good and so many Gentlemen's seats round it, that a stranger may pleasantly pass away a week here.' The 2nd Earl of Oxford, in *A Journey in the Eastern Counties December 1737-January 1738*, remarked that, 'it has been much rebuilt of late years …'. He noted that the 'churchyard is well planted, the walks gravelled, this is the Mall for the beaux and belles of Chelmsford'. He mentions the conduit which 'never fails, and fine water it is. There are the Duke of Albermarle's [*sic*] Arms and Fitzwalter; I suppose they contributed to bring the water to the place … We lay at the Ipswich Arms, but an indifferent inn.' This inn, approximately on the site of what is now the Meadows shopping precinct, was later used as the Assize Judge's lodging and was described as wretched, the roof not keeping the rain out and not 'consistent with the dignity and opulence of the County'.

In July the Rev. Charles Lyttleton, Rector of Alvechurch, on a journey from Ealing to Norfolk, wrote to a friend: 'A Publick conduit which supplies the Town at Chelmsford runs a hogshead and a half from three spouts every minute and consequently between eight and nine thousand hogsheads in a year.' A hogshead equals 52½ imperial gallons.

41 The Mildmay Almshouses in Moulsham Street founded by Thomas Mildmay in 1565. From an original drawing by Derek Wilks.

The Earl of Oxford no doubt had his own equipage but others used the public coach service established in the 1730s. There were daily coaches to London and a mail coach passed through the town twice each day. An issue of the *Ipswich Journal* advised:

> This is to give notice that a handsome machine, with steel springs for the ease of passengers and the conveniency of the County, begins on Monday 8th July 1754 to set off from Chelmsford every morning at 7 o'clock, Sunday excepted, to the Bull Inn, Leadenhall Street to be there by 12 o'clock and to return the same day at 2 o'clock to be at Chelmsford by 7 o'clock in the evening.

In 1730 the maintenance of roads was the responsibility of householders, except in Moulsham where help was given by the Essex Turnpike Trust, set up in 1726, and it was possible for surveyors to collect a highways rate. Labourers were paid to maintain the roads by means of 'Shovel Money', which most householders preferred to pay to avoid statutory labour. Sometimes inmates of the workhouse were employed on these duties.

A workhouse had been established in 1716 substituting for several almshouses on different sites, including four in Moulsham, which also had the Mildmay Almshouses in Moulsham Street. These dated from 1616, though the site had previously been used for charitable purposes: there had been a leper hospital there from before 1293. The Mildmay Almshouses were rebuilt in 1758 and residence there now is in the gift of Chelmsford United Charities, on which there are two church representatives and six Borough Council members. There is a residency qualification of two years in Chelmsford. The rebuilding is noted on a plaque, easily seen from the pavement: 'Founded by THOMAS MILDMAY Esq of Moulsham Hall 1565 Rebuilt by WILLIAM MILDMAY 1758'.

The new workhouse was set up to cater to the needs of the local destitute or homeless and those unfortunate enough to be disabled, orphaned, infirm or aged. Three meals per day were provided, some using vegetables grown in the garden. 'They have all a clean shift every week, and care is taken that they be washed and their hair combed.' Work was provided in the garden, on domestic chores, and in spinning and wool-carding. From 1751, hemp and sacks were manufactured, an enterprise which flourished and made a profit. In that year 50 men, women and children were living at the workhouse, including the master, his wife and their four children.

Also introduced for the benefit of the poor was a charity school. Established in 1713, the school aimed to educate and clothe 50 boys and 30 girls and was made possible by the subscriptions of local people and a donation from the magistrates' bench of £30. Although there had been schools in the latter part of the previous century, this was the first permanent school for the poor, and original funds were supplemented by collections at meetings. The enterprise was supported by the rector, Oliver Pocklington, who was holder of that post for 33 years from 1706. At first at 71 High Street, the school moved to New Street in 1724 and offered reading, psalmody, writing and arithmetic. The girls also learned knitting and the making of clothes, fitting them to enter service in due course.

Apart from volunteer officers such as churchwardens and overseers of the poor, in 1730 a beadle was employed at £4 per annum. In his uniform and official hat he patrolled the area and delivered orders and messages. In 1742 an engineer was engaged to take charge of two fire engines, purchased in 1731 and housed at the parish church, which had supplemented buckets, ladders and hooks, all vital equipment in the face of the ever-present danger of fire.

From 1738, attempts were made to formalise the medical care of the poor by contracting apothecaries on an annual salary. In 1747, one of those appointed was Dr Benjamin Pugh, who subsequently built the Mansion House in the High Street, later the offices of the *Weekly News* and Royal Bank of Scotland, which still graces the street today. Pugh was a pioneer in the fields of midwifery and inoculation for smallpox, a disease which was rampant in the town in the early 1750s when there were hundreds of cases. His interest in the town also took in the county gaol.

At the summer Assizes of 1767, the condition of the county gaol was criticised and an 18-man committee was established to determine what should be done. George Dance, a surveyor who was later to become Clerk of the City Works, London, was asked to investigate rebuilding on the same site. After considering other locations, he recommended that the original 'Old Spot' to the west of the road next to the river on the Moulsham side be reused, with the addition of some 'small pieces of ground'. He concluded that sewage and other waste could be disposed of into the river, that there was a good fresh-water supply, and that the positioning would not, unlike other options in the town, affect local residents too much.

42 Chelmsford Goal and House of Correction beside the Stone Bridge in Moulsham, *c.*1805. Cattle and sheep are being driven down what was still the main road to London. The soldiers on the bridge are a few of the many stationed here in the early 19th century.

Thus began a protracted and acrimonious argument between a group led by Bamber Gascoigne of Barking, Member of Parliament for Midhurst, Sussex, who wished the gaol to be removed to a position closer to the court house (and drafted a Bill for the purpose), and Sir William Mildmay, who led a Town Petition for the gaol to remain where it was and where it did not interfere with private property or the market or fairs. Sir William did offer a site that he owned in New Street as an alternative but a Bill passed its third reading in April 1770 allowing the rebuilding on the Moulsham site. Gascoigne, however, pursued a site at No. 1 High Street, the *White Horse Inn*, as part of a plan which envisaged a new court house on the site opposite the inn with

function rooms for social purposes as well as spaces for judicial matters. A meeting of justices chaired by him in September approved the site and the amendment of the Bill. A petition supporting this amendment was opposed by five counter-petitions from local people.

Dr Pugh, in evidence to a parliamentary committee, indicated that the *White Horse* site, on the corner of Waterloo Lane, would require a water supply, presumably from the conduit. This would interfere with the town supply which he said cleansed the town, running as it did down the principal street, supplied water for the extinguishing of fires and prevented the air from stagnating in the High Street, which was of benefit to the health of

43 The impressive Palladian façade of Moulsham Hall in the mid-18th century after years of rebuilding. The house was demolished in 1809.

residents! He and other witnesses prevailed and, despite further manoeuvres by Gascoigne, work proceeded in Moulsham, prisoners moving to other parts of the old gaol while demolition and rebuilding carried on around them. The new gaol was completed after four years' work in 1777 at the cost of £15,000. It was an impressive stone building, looking more like a private mansion than a prison, but it was poorly ventilated, lacked bathing facilities and provision for the sick and had cramped sleeping quarters, which meant that prisoners were too crowded at night. Figures for July 1782 show that there were 47 prisoners, both felons and debtors.

The House of Correction in the High Street, opposite the corner of Springfield Road, was for the detention of tramps and others who would not or could not conform. Built in the 1750s and 1760s to a poor standard, it was rebuilt next to the new gaol, to the design of John Johnson, County Surveyor from 1782 to 1812 and completed in 1806 at the cost of £7,390. Johnson was also responsible for remedial work at the gaol required by an Act of 1784, which gave separate accommodation for different sexes and classes of prisoner. The drains were improved and a bath for prisoners was provided.

Sir William Mildmay had succeeded to the Mildmay estates in 1756 on the death of Benjamin Mildmay, 19th and final Baron Fitzwalter. The century had begun during the incumbency of Charles Mildmay, who died childless in 1728, having been lord of both manors for nearly fifty years. He passed on the Fitzwalter barony to Benjamin Mildmay, his brother, who had been, between 1706-8, equerry to Queen Anne's husband, the 'amiable nonentity', Prince George of Denmark.

Benjamin married well, to Frederica, daughter of the Duke of Schomberg and cousin to King George I. She had a fine property in Pall Mall, London.

Benjamin Mildmay took an active part in local affairs, being the rector's warden, an overseer of the poor, Lord Lieutenant and Custos Rotulorum. He was also a governor of King Edward VI Grammar School. Between 1728 and 1743, his principal occupation was the rebuilding of Moulsham Hall, which may have acted as a stimulus to refurbishing and rebuilding in the High Street. He employed Giacomo Leoni to replace the standing Tudor buildings with a two-storey mansion in Palladian style, each section in its turn being demolished and rebuilt. When it was complete, the house had an impressive frontage decorated with lead statues of Apollo, Diana and Mercury. The rebuilding gave work to many local craftsmen and was remarked upon by the Earl of Oxford: 'From hence [Ingatestone Hall], we went for Chelmsford. Within a mile we left Moulsham on the right hand, it is my Lord Fitzwalter's, he has laid out money upon it.' The site of the house lies approximately in the area of the present Moulsham Infant and Junior Schools.

This was property which Sir William Mildmay inherited. He was a descendant of the first Thomas Mildmay's brother, William of Springfield Barnes, but was not of the Fitzwalter line. He was a traveller and linguist who had performed diplomatic duties in North America, the West Indies and France. As we have seen, he too took an interest in the town and within two years of succeeding he had rebuilt the Mildmay Almshouses in Moulsham Street. When he died in 1771, he left a bequest of £200 in trust to be invested for the repair and cleaning of pipes from the Burgess Well to the conduit and any other work necessary to secure the provision of a clean and wholesome water supply. His widow, Ann, survived for a further 25 years as lady of the twin manors.

During the lives of her two predecessors as lords of the manors, the High Street had been transformed from a medieval town to a 'modern' one. The site of 13/14 High Street, for example, was refronted with brick c.1740, as was the site of 42/3 in the late 1750s. The *Black Boy Inn* on the north corner of Springfield Road was rebuilt in the middle of the century and Thomas Clapham built a three-storey mansion on the site of 65/6 in the late 1760s. The *White Horse*, the alternative site for the county gaol, was pulled down in 1776 and replaced with two brick-built private houses. Peter Muilman, a rich London merchant of Dutch descent, saw Chelmsford in 1771 as 'having four streets, but is beautiful, regular and well built'. The High Street had 'many handsome, good houses'. He found that

What contributes much to the peculiar cleanliness of this town is its being gravelled ... The sign posts which formerly used to project out so as to be a very glaring nuisance are now entirely removed ... The Chelmer and Can form here an angle along which lie many pleasure gardens etc ... On the banks of these rivers various temples and summer houses are built some of which are so pretty in their construction as to display an elegance of taste in their projectors.

The culmination of these and many other improvements lay at either end of the High Street. The poor condition of the Stone Bridge or Great Bridge, built in 1372, had caused considerable concern in the 18th century because of both the volume of traffic using it and the effects of regular flooding upon its structure. By 1670, the county had accepted responsibility for its maintenance but it was not until the end of the 18th century that the

44 Moulsham or Stone Bridge from a postcard of *c.*1900, showing the elegant sweep of John Johnson's architecture.

magistrates decided to replace it. Instead of having two piers, as formerly, a single arch bridge was planned with a span of 34 feet and a footway on either side. In 1761 a wooden footbridge had been constructed for pedestrians but this had been closed in 1784 because of its parlous condition. In October 1785 work on the new brick construction began and it was opened in January 1788, though its keystone is dated 1787. Portland stone was used for its finish and an artificial material, Coade stone, was used both for decorative purposes (four paterae with the head of a river god), and for the 72 balusters making up a safety rail. It is possible today to see the different wear on these materials compared with those used for the main structure. Only one baluster is not original. One fell into the river during the 19th century and was recovered during flood relief work by the Essex River Board in the 1960s. It was donated to the Chelmsford and Essex Museum.

Problems were later caused by the narrowing of the river from 54 feet to 36 feet to accommodate the bridge's span. No less than Thomas Telford was called in to advise in 1824. Of his two recommendations, only one was carried out: to clear the channel and allow a better flow of water. Fortunately the second, to replace the bridge with a cast-iron one, was turned down and John Johnson's bridge still graces the town. Now a foot-bridge with the irregular flow of service traffic, it has survived not only the farm carts, wagons and carriages

45   The keystone of the bridge showing the date 1787, although the bridge actually opened for traffic in January 1788.

46   A patera attached to the bridge showing the head of a river god, made in Coade stone, supplied by the Lambeth factory of Mrs Eleanor Coade.

for which it was built but also the depredations of double-decker buses, pantechnicons and articulated lorries.

In the early 18th century the Great Cross, built in 1569, was the building used for criminal justice cases and the Little Cross for civil cases. Both were sited at the top of the High Street. The former, also termed the Sessions House, was at this time in a decaying state. In 1714 the Little Cross was demolished and rebuilt and the Great Cross was extensively restored. In the dispute over the siting of the county gaol Bamber Gascoigne had raised the matter of a new court building, and in October 1788

47 John Johnson, County Surveyor of Essex 1782-1812, who was responsible for the building and improving Chelmsford Gaol and House of Correction, the Stone Bridge and Shire Hall and the rebuilding of the parish church.

Quarter Sessions decided that the current structures were not 'in a fit condition for transacting the publick business of the County' and called for a report.

Three sites were considered, as was the refurbishment of the standing structures. It was finally decided to demolish both Crosses and acquire some private parcels of land in order to reuse the same site for new buildings on a plan drawn up by John Johnson. Work commenced

in 1789 and the acquired buildings were pulled down; the court houses, however, remained so that courts could continue to sit, much to the annoyance of building contractors. The new structure of three storeys and five bays with three arched entrances was faced in Portland stone and displayed three personifications, Justice, Wisdom and Mercy, executed in Coade stone above three windows, each between a total of four Ionic columns. It had two large courts, rooms for county business and a 'capital ballroom', first used for an assembly in October 1791. The furnishing of this room was paid for by county-wide public subscription and included a contribution of £20 from Dame Ann Mildmay.

The courts themselves were first used in July 1791. The entrance area was used on market days and fair days by farmers, particularly for dealing in corn. Space was also provided for the storage of stalls. The area was, however, small, inconvenient and badly illuminated, and in 1857 was replaced by a purpose-built Corn Exchange.

As the power of the manor courts leet declined and the sway of the magistracy increased, as we have seen with the construction of the Shire Hall and the bridge, a gap in public business encompassing by-laws and the control of public nuisances grew. Although the manor courts still fined wrong-doers, inhabitants of Chelmsford in the 1780s were beginning to press for better paving, lighting and watching, particularly after a spate of thefts and burglaries. A petition signed by 95 leading residents including the rector, the Reverend John Morgan, incumbent from 1774-1817, requested a clause in the Shire Hall parliamentary bill in 1788 but eventually promoted their own bill for the purpose, which became an Act in 1789. The Act's provisions allowed the appointment

48   The Shire Hall from a painting by Philip Reinagle. 'To Thomas Berney Bramston, John Bullock Esq. Knights of the Shire and the other magistrates of the County of Essex This view of the County Hall at Chelmsford is inscribed by their most obedient servant John Johnson'.

49   Plaques in Coade stone on the façade of the Shire Hall, illustrating Justice, Wisdom and Mercy. The clock in the pediment, known to all Chelmsfordians today, was the gift of Sparrows Bank to commemorate the Golden Jubilee of Queen Victoria in 1887. From an original drawing by Derek Wilks.

50 The Coade stone Naiad in the Shire Hall. She originally stood outside the Hall.

a brewer and included such men as William Clachar, Dr Henry Menish and John Oxley Parker, steward of the manor. The role of chief pledges virtually passed into history. As well as the power to fine those who caused nuisances, by, for example, obstructing the footways, they employed night watchmen who were empowered to make arrests. Paving of the east side of the High Street, the other side being gravelled, started in 1790 as did the erection of street lighting.

In 1791 or 1792, with the help of Sir William Mildmay's bequest and donations by the public and the Royal Exchange and Sun Fire Offices, an improved flow of water to the conduit was achieved. John Johnson designed a figure of a Greek nymph almost six feet high, a Naiad leaning on a shield on a cylinder decorated with four dolphins. Mounted on a five-foot-high hollow pillar, its surface is rusticated. At the base, water poured from the mouths of four lion's heads. The whole assemblage was produced in Coade stone and complemented the new Shire Hall but only until 1814, when a domed rotunda replaced it, itself to be replaced by the statue of Nicholas Tindal in 1851. The domed structure moved to the centre of the High Street at the corner of Springfield Road in 1852 but, because of increased traffic levels, moved again to Tower Gardens in 1940, where it can still be seen. The Naiad disappeared from view for many years, later standing in the garden of Dr Aubrey from the 1870s until 1963, when she was donated to the Borough Council, who placed it on display in the Chelmsford and Essex Museum. Finally she was moved to the front hall of the Shire Hall in 1980 after conservation work had been completed. Over the years the Naiad has lost her shield, much of her right and some of her left arms, and a large section of her nose.

of 50 commissioners appointed for life, with the surveyors and rector *ex officio*. The commissioners, who were subject to a property qualification, comprised, among others, doctors, lawyers, shop-owners, licensed victuallers and

The completion of the Shire Hall provided a further venue for public meetings in the town. At the end of the century the *Saracen's Head* and the *Black Boy* amongst others continued to provide large-scale accommodation, the former for such 'entertainments' as cock-fighting, the latter particularly attracting passing trade. The *Ipswich Express* noted: '... between forty and fifty stage coaches passed its door daily, most of which pulled up, if they did not pause to allow travellers to partake of the provision made for them; while numberless pairs of post horses stood saddled in its capacious stables'. Both could provide space for between two and three hundred people to attend concerts, assemblies and balls or view plays such as *The Merry Midnight Mistake*, *The Harlot's Progress*, *School for Scandal* and various works of Shakespeare. William Clachar, an expatriate Scot, opened a theatre in 1790, approximately on the site of the modern Marks & Spencer, which was also used as an auction room. In 1795, the *Chelmsford Chronicle* reported that the theatre was 'a resort of fashion, respect and elegance'.

A wider range of entertainment was available during the three-day Chelmsford Races at Galleywood, established in 1759, which continued in to the 20th century, the last race meeting taking place in 1935. Parts of the course barrier are still visible today. There were also clubs and societies. Cricket was played from 1755. There was a bowling green behind the *White Horse Inn* until 1776. Bear-baiting was still carried on and a 'Flowerists' Feast was held every July. The Chelmsford Beef-Steak Club was set up in 1768 and still exists today. Meeting at the *Black Boy*, and later at the *Saracen's Head*, its membership was restricted to 40 gentlemen and its monthly meetings took place on the Friday nearest to the full moon, eminently practical when members had to travel

51 Half penny token of 1794 issued by William Clachar with the edge inscription: Payable at Clachar Co's Chelmsford Essex.

home in the dark to such homes as Springfield Place, Writtle Lodge, Danbury Park or Hedingham Castle. The restricted numbers meant that those selected as members formed a very exclusive clique of highly influential people belonging to the landed gentry, the clergy, the armed forces and the professions. Perhaps it is not surprising that James Boswell, in 1792, described Chelmsford as 'this capital of the County of Essex'.

On 10 August 1764 the first edition of the *Chelmsford Chronicle* or *Essex Weekly Advertiser* appeared. It is still the major mid-Essex newspaper today, issued under the title *Essex*

52 Front page of the first edition of the *Chelmsford Chronicle* or *Essex Weekly Advertiser*, now known as the *Essex Chronicle*. It remains one of the oldest businesses in the county.

53 Perspective view of the County Town of Essex 1762 by David Ogbourne, showing the procession of Assize judges, preceded by trumpeters and pike men to the Sessions House. A fiddler leans against the *Red Lion* inn sign and many watch from the windows of their elegant new or refronted houses. The High Street has lost its medieval look.

Chronicle. The paper's first leader stated that, 'It has often been thought surprising that the County of Essex, which is one of the most considerable in England, should be without a newspaper, the source of information and the channel of intelligence.' It went on to declare that it would not be simply a newspaper but a 'FAMILY LIBRARY'. Certainly the first edition contained wide-ranging items, for example on Count Poniatowsky, Ode Nine from the Third Book of Horace, a report from St Petersburg and another on the bankruptcy of a Liverpool druggist. There is also local news: 'Wednesday The Right Honourable Lord Mansfield and the Honourable Mr. Baron Smythe made their entrance to the town and yesterday the Assizes began before Lord Mansfield.' There are advertisements including one for Chelmsford Races on 20 August and another for William Myers, staymaker:

> This is to inform the ladies of the County in particular his original customers that he is restored to his former health and hopes the continuance of their favours as they will know his experience and workmanship. All letters ... shall be carefully and punctually observed by their obedient humble servant William Myers.

BROWN & SON, Ltd., CHELMSFORD.
(Established 1798)

All Classes of English and Foreign Timber
Sawn & Planed Goods - Poles - Doors, Mldgs,
Etc.,   Etc.,
Delivery by Road direct to site.

54 Advertisement for Brown & Son Ltd showing the extent of their timber supply business, which continued until the 1970s, a period of almost two hundred years.

There was also gossip: 'A few days ago, a man at Brentwood attempting to drink a large quantity of Geneva, fell off his chair and expired immediately.' Geneva is a spirit distilled from grain and flavoured with juniper berries.

The town boasted many businesses. There were perukemakers and hairdressers, milliners, drapers, hatters, haberdashers and shoemakers. In her listing of businesses in the High Street in the early 1790s, Hilda Grieve included nine drapers, seven tailors, three staymakers, one stay and ladies' riding-habit maker and two glove and breeches makers. Then, as now, Chelmsford was a retail centre for all manner of finished goods as well as those associated with the various aspects of agriculture. There were, for example, four watchmakers and, to handle the wealth of business, a bank was established by Charles Alexander Crickitt and Dr Henry Menish in March 1790. Both these men were to support another new venture.

Between them, the bridge and the Shire Hall had required many tons of Portland stone and other materials, often imported at Maldon and laboriously brought cross-country and over Danbury Hill on usually atrocious roads. Hundreds of tons of coal and other commodities were similarly transported by wagon or pack-animal each year. It had been suggested for many years that bulk items including timber could more easily and cheaply be carried by water, first by Andrew Yarranton in the 1670s, and the idea was resurrected in 1733 and then again in 1762. William Mildmay, following a survey of the River Chelmer by Thomas Yeoman, sought financial backing for a canal scheme. An Act of Parliament was passed in 1766, but it had been opposed by the borough of Maldon, for fear of losing tolls on wagons passing through the town, and by landowners who were disturbed by the possibility that their waters, for powering mills for example, might be interrupted. The scheme failed, however, because insufficient funds were accrued, despite the backing of Mildmay and Lord Petre of Ingatestone.

A new navigation canal scheme, again backed by the Petre family, now joined by Dame Ann Mildmay, Thomas Berney Bramston of Skreens, Roxwell, Charles Crickitt and Henry Menish, William Clachar and many others in Chelmsford, was brought to fruition in an Act

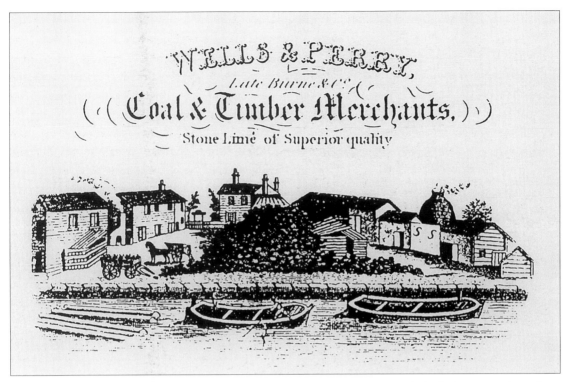

55 Advertisement for Wells & Perry, who also owned a brewery, later the Chelmsford Brewery, in Duke Street, now the site of Dukes. In the foreground are open barges used for transporting heavy goods from the sea to the town at Springfield Basin. This area now contains residential buildings and recreational facilities.

of Parliament in February 1793. Work took four years and suffered from lack of capital but was eventually completed in 1797. The navigation was 13¾ miles long and had 12 locks plus a sea-lock at Heybridge. The river was widened, straightened and deepened, thereby allowing barges of sixty feet in length, with a beam of fourteen feet, to pass. Wharves were built to serve communities along the banks and a basin and wharfage were created at Springfield under the direction of John Rennie and his resident engineer, Richard Coates.

Work had begun at Heybridge, where the first ship docked in April 1796, and proceeded incrementally towards Chelmsford. The navigation was opened in June 1797 by barges laden with coal, with their 'colours flying'. The ability to transport heavy loads of coal

into Chelmsford led to the establishment in 1819 of gas works by the Chelmsford Gas, Light and Coke Company and the illumination of the town's streets from October 1819. With the one in Colchester, this was the first gas works in the county. In 1836, Thomas Wright remarked, 'The town is well lighted with gas, derived from the works at Springfield.'

Edmund Durrant, shopkeeper and instigator of the *Essex Review*, wrote at the end of the 19th century,

> When the first barge arrived from Maldon, the event was celebrated by a public holiday and the inhabitants gave themselves up to all kinds of amusement. Chelmsford was illuminated and bonfires were lighted in all directions. Considering however that the canal cost £50,000 and that it paid no dividend for twenty year, I am afraid that the persons who became so hilarious on that occasion did not reap much to repay them for all that excitement.

Although the navigation continued to bring coal to Chelmsford until 1927 and timber to Brown & Sons of Navigation Road until 1972 (a business, incidentally, started by Richard Coates' nephew, James Brown), its busiest period was, ironically, when carrying materials for the Eastern Counties Railway in the 1840s. The opening of the railway line to Chelmsford in 1843 started the gradual decline of the navigation. Its revival in the last quarter of the 20th century has been brought about by the introduction of narrow boats, the activities of the Chelmsford Canoe Club, the Sea Cadets, the Inland Waterways Association and the Friends of the Chelmer and Blackwater Navigation, formed in 1996.

The 18th century brought change and enhancement to the county town, but the following century was to bring greater and more far-reaching changes to its inhabitants.

Four

Perspectives Change

Chelmsford church and Writtle steeple
Fell down one day
But killed no people

Anonymous

The collapse of the nave of the parish church in 1800, mirrored by the fall of part of the steeple at Writtle, a village to the west of the town, was recorded in the doggerel of the time. These events, right at the beginning of the century, seem to symbolise the changes to come, with the collapse of the old and the introduction of the new. The momentous changes of the 19th century in Chelmsford were particularly felt in relation to the changing balance of wealth creation, which was to be evident by its closing years. The century also witnessed improvements in local government and public health, culminating in the incorporation of the town in 1888, followed by the creation of the Essex County Council, based in Chelmsford, in 1889. The coming of the railway brought not only easier and quicker access to the rest of the county at large and to the capital, but it also acted as a spur for new

56 Embroidery by Mary Stevens showing the parish church with a hot-air balloon floating past. The Department of Textiles, Victoria & Albert Museum date it to *c.*1810, which coincides with a balloon ascent by James Sadler in August 1811. The 'flags' may be paddles which were believed to aid the balloon's flight.

57 Several views of the collapse of St Mary's Church in 1800 exist, enlivened with men working or with visitors, including military figures, examining the devastation, almost as though they were classical ruins.

industry, starting the move away from Chelmsford's dependence on agriculture as the principal source of the town's income.

The cost of rebuilding the parish church, which took three years, was borne not only by those who used the established church but by those who did not. The latter were to mark their divergence from the orthodox and their emergence as a potent force in the middle of the century by building a new thoroughfare

58 Interior of the church in 1851 showing Johnson's delicate work with Coade stone both in the ceiling and the font, now at Chelmsford Museum. The pews, pulpit and altar have all been replaced.

into the town, which included the first post-Reformation Roman Catholic church, a strict Baptist church, a Congregational church and a non-denominational cemetery.

The parish church fell down because workmen digging within the church to lay to rest a local notable were too near one of the pillars supporting the roof, with the result that, on the evening of Friday 17 January, the columns of the south arcade collapsed into the hole and brought down the roof, the south aisle and part of the north aisle. The task of rebuilding

59 Captain George Cheveley of the Roxwell Volunteers, *c.*1805. Captain Cheveley, of Boyton Hall, Roxwell, was also a member of the influential Chelmsford Beef-Steak Club.

60 A Private of the Loyal Chelmsford Volunteers depicted on a tea tray. The troop was raised in 1798 by Captain Thomas Frost Gepp, attorney, of Maynetrees and comprised a Captain, 1st Lieutenant, 2nd Lieutenant, Sergeant Major, two Sergeants, one Corporal and 36 privates.

the church fell to John Johnson, the builder of the new bridge at Moulsham and the Shire Hall at the head of the High Street. Again Johnson used the ubiquitous Coade stone, in the gothic tracery of the roof of the building, the arcade and the clerestory windows and for a font subsequently passed to St Peter's, the 'tin church' in Primrose Hill. While the church was being rebuilt, which took three and a half years, services were held in the Shire Hall.

The collapse of the church would be a momentous event at any time but in a period when most people would contemplate only local matters, and even those who could read

and could afford a newspaper would tend to concentrate on parochial concerns, its occurrence was seen as significant. The town also experienced the upheaval of troops being quartered here on an unprecedented scale. They were en route to the Channel ports or were building, maintaining and manning substantial earthworks to the south-east of the town. Hilda Grieve has noted that during the Revolutionary Wars between April 1793 and April 1794, 179 commissioned officers and 8,304 non-commissioned officers and men with 627 horses were billeted in the town. In October 1798, 5,000 troops were stationed in Chelmsford and

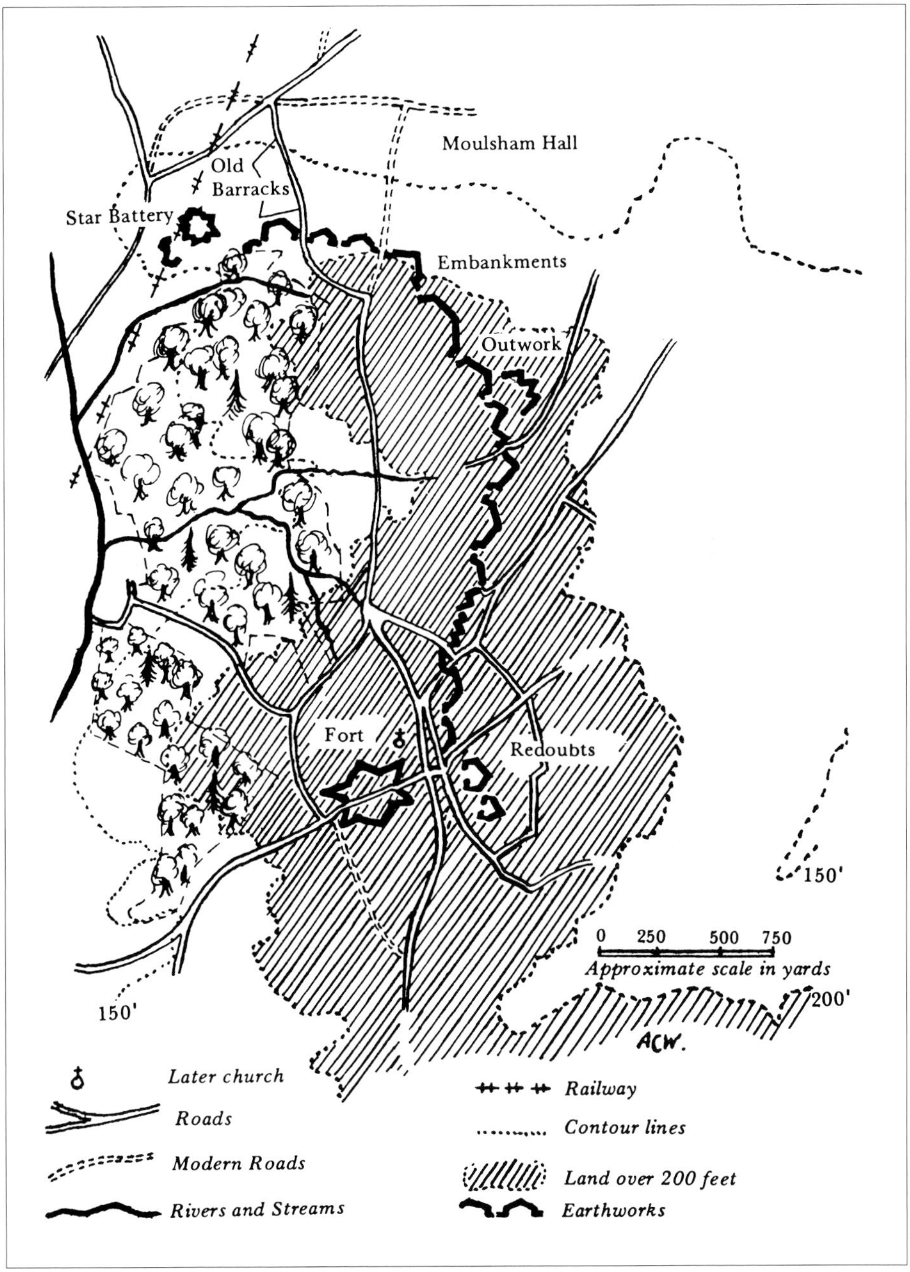

61 Plan of the substantial defences built *c.*1803 to defend the approaches to Chelmsford. Thousands of men would have been needed to man these defences if Napoleon's troops had invaded. Lady Mildmay was upset by the earthworks so close to her property at Moulsham Hall. From an original drawing by Arthur Wright.

Moulsham Hall

Star Battery

Old Barracks

Embankments

Outwork

Fort

Redoubts

150'

0   250   500   750

Approximate scale in yards

150'

200'

ACW.

        Later church

        Roads

        Modern Roads

        Rivers and Streams

        Railway

        Contour lines

        Land over 200 feet

        Earthworks

Moulsham, again outnumbering the towns-people, the population according to the census of 1801 being 3,755. There were also the forces of volunteers; the Loyal Chelmsford Volunteers and the Roxwell Volunteers were part of this band, raised mostly by local gentry to act as a domestic defence force in the case of invasion by the forces of Napoleon.

Some of the soldiers were used in the excavation of extensive earthworks and the building of batteries in the Widford and Galleywood areas, which were to defend the

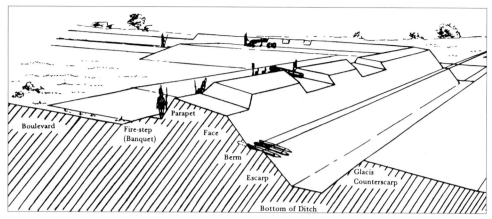

62 Perspective and section of the earthworks which ran from Wood Street to Galleywood Common. Each end of the Lines was enhanced with a Star Fort, mounted with ordnance. Virtually all traces of the defences have been destroyed. From an original drawing by Arthur Wright.

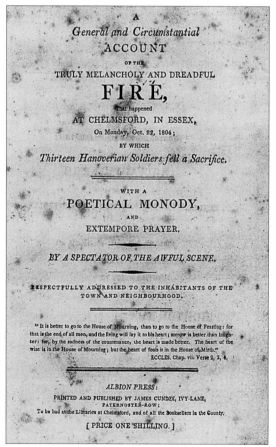

63 Pamphlet issued to mark the tragic fire of October 1804. The soldiers who died were buried in a common grave in the churchyard.

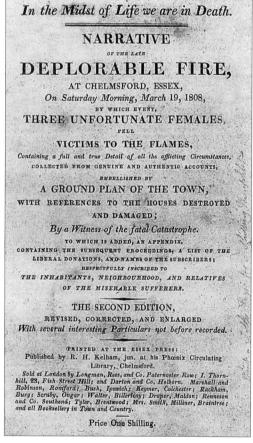

64 Pamphlet issued after 'the late Deplorable Fire at Chelmsford' in March 1808, which prompted concern about the congestion of some of the town's buildings.

principal approaches to the county town. Some signs of their existence can still be seen in Galleywood but the barracks already existing in the Wood Street area, once called Barrack Lane, and the new ones at Coval Lane have left no trace of their existence. In 1823 the products of their demolition were being sold as building materials. A military presence continued in the town and the demolition of the county gaol in 1859 led to the building of military installations in the area next to the river on the Moulsham side of the Stone Bridge which is still known as Barrack Square. Here was the depot of the West Essex Militia. Chelmsford's first mayor, Frederic Chancellor, was an early volunteer when the second Napoleon threatened Britain. He left the force as a Lieutenant Colonel.

The earthworks gave Lady Jane Mildmay the opportunity to relieve herself of the burden imposed upon her under the will of her late aunt, which required her to spend three months of the year at Moulsham Hall. The property was not in a good state of repair, because of damp caused by a poor roof, and she leased the hall for four years to the General Officer commanding the area. When the property was returned to her its condition had deteriorated and, in 1808, it was demolished, the contents being subsequently sold for £1,661 and the building materials for £4,470. Although at least one member of the Mildmay family was to play a leading role in the 19th-century development of Chelmsford, and local people were to continue to benefit from the family connection, the loss of a lady of the manor in residence changed a state of affairs which had obtained from the mid-16th century.

Soldiers were involved in one of the two disastrous fires in the town in the first decade of the 19th century. In 1804, 13 Hanoverian

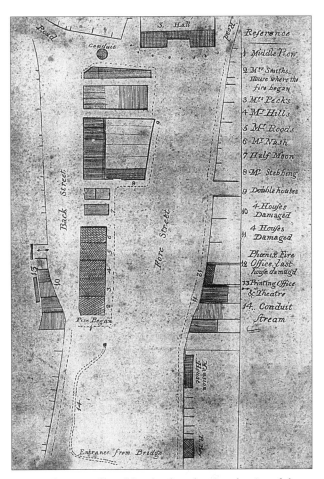

65 The area affected by the fire, showing the site of the *Half Moon Inn*, the theatre and the conduit.

soldiers were burnt to death at the rear of the *Spotted Dog* public house in Tindal Street. Billeted in the stables, it is believed they were unfamiliar both with the type of catch used on a door they were unable to release and the language, being part of a force from the German possessions of the British Crown. In 1808, 'the lives of three unfortunate females fell victims to the flames' of another conflagration in Tindal Street and parts of the High Street. A contemporary pamphlet describing the catastrophe was 'respectfully inscribed to the inhabitants, neighbourhood and relatives to the miserable sufferers'. The

66 The tomb of 'the three unfortunate females' in the cathedral churchyard: Mary Ann Woolmer, Mary Elizabeth Eve and Mary Smith, the last a milliner whose house was destroyed and the former her two apprentices.

67 Although George IV was not a popular monarch, very few people would have remembered the coronation celebrations of his father, George III, sixty years before. They would be aware, no doubt, of their new King's sponsorship of Chelmsford Races. Chelmsford therefore took the opportunity to mark the day with music, fireworks and 'other demonstrations of joy' on 19 July 1821.

gravestone commemorating the deaths can still be seen in the cathedral churchyard, giving the rather sombre advice: 'Prepare for death ere ye retire to rest. For ye know not what a day may bring forth.'

The chief source of wealth of the town was agriculture and its myriad offshoots, and in 1824 there were five surgeons, four tailors, three watchmakers, six attorneys, four chemists and druggists and seven fire office agents amongst many others. The town's many licensed premises thrived both on these concerns and on the passing trade, but it was the latter that was to change forever in the

middle part of the century. Railway 'mania' showed itself in Essex, the main railway line being the one driven through the county town towards Colchester and the east coast. Passenger services started in Chelmsford in 1843. An anonymous article in the *Essex Review* of 1900 showed that early railway travel, though more convenient and faster, had its disadvantages: 'I remember travelling from Witham to Chelmsford in 1843 in an open railway carriage, that is with no roof, sides or windows and with seats for passengers resembling forms, built on the floor of the truck.' An unknown poet writing in the 1840s

68 Apart from the ladies and gentlemen milling about watching 'a thousand of the poor dine ... precisely at One o'clock' at two long tables in the High Street, many others view the scene of the coronation celebrations from their windows.

was clearly impressed with the new railway viaduct and with the locomotives:

And yonder where in close succession rise
Arch after arch inviting our surprise,
There runs the railway – hark! that piercing cry
The engine with its ponderous train draws nigh;
Onward it comes with twenty horses power
With speed at rate of fifty miles per hour.

One victim of the rapid diminution of stage-coaches passing through the town was the *Black Boy Inn* which, according to the *Ipswich Express* in the year the inn was demolished, 1857, had been a busy venue. *Pigot's Directory* of 1839

noted that the Royal Mail from Norwich called every morning at 3 a.m., the Telegraph from Great Yarmouth at 4.15 a.m., the Coggeshall Coach at 9 a.m. and the Wellington from Colchester at 11.30 a.m. Charles Dickens referred to the inn in *The Pickwick Papers*, where Sam Weller's father says: 'I worked down the wery day arter the night you caught the rheumatiz,and at the Black Boy in Chelmsford ... I took 'em up, right through to Ipswich.' Dickens himself said of Chelmsford in 1854 that it was 'the dullest and most stupid spot on earth' and this view was echoed by a

69 Richard Clay, night watchman, *c*.1827. After the fires of 1804 and 1808 the number of watchmen was increased from two to four, but the posts ceased after the county police took on the ancient function of watch and ward in 1840.

Mr Copland of Bellefield, New London Road, writing to his brother Theodore in November 1857: 'Here is a warning for you. There is great paucity of news in this dead alive town.'

Anthony Trollope, however, seemed to like the town and stayed at the *Saracen's Head* on a number of occasions either in his capacity as

Inspector General of the Post Office or for hunting. He wrote parts of some of the Barchester novels while in residence. The novels were produced in weekly parts and Fred Spalding mentioned in his reminiscences that Trollope was seated in the *Saracen's Head* on one occasion when

> two clergymen entered having purchased across the street the last number of Barchester Towers. Hastily cutting it open, one of them ran his eye down the pages. 'Confound that Mrs Proudie,' he exclaimed, 'I wish she were dead.' The reader in the distance looked up. 'Gentlemen,' he quietly remarked, 'she shall die in the next number.' The surprise of the visitors at discovering themselves in the presence of Mrs Proudie's creator may be imagined.

The Eastern Counties Railway were able to lay their track through the town and beyond following the sale of the necessary land by the Mildmay family. The first Mildmay had entailed his properties in Chelmsford to the male line but legislation in the 1830s allowed the family to conclude a number of settlements which allowed land to be sold. The railway benefited directly from such sales but a second and equally significant sale, which took place on four days in May 1839, led to the building of New London Road, the first in the town to have planning restrictions applied to it. Land was purchased by or on behalf of a group of gentlemen, brought together by family ties, business interests and nonconformist religious conviction, who were known as the Chelmsford Company. Their number included John Copland, a solicitor, William Collings Wells, a brewer, Thomas Greenwood, a banker, Edward Copland, John's son, and James Fenton, an architect and engineer. High standards were imposed by covenants on buildings in the new street, which featured a mixture of terraced properties, semi-detached and detached residences built of white brick, stone or cemented

70 The calendar of the Lent Assize, Chelmsford 1835. Assizes were held twice a year at Lent and summer and dealt with serious criminal and civil cases. Quarter Sessions met at Epiphany, Easter or Lent, Midsummer and Michaelmas to hear less serious cases and undertake administrative matters.

ESSEX.

GAOL CALENDAR,

FOR

THE LENT ASSIZE,

HOLDEN

On MONDAY, the 9th of MARCH, 1835, at CHELMSFORD,

BEFORE

THE RIGHT HONORABLE THOMAS LORD DENMAN,

CHIEF JUSTICE OF THE COURT OF KING'S BENCH;

AND

THE HONORABLE SIR STEPHEN GASELEE, KNIGHT,

ONE OF THE JUSTICES OF OUR LORD THE KING, OF THE COURT OF COMMON PLEAS.

GEORGE WILLIAM GENT, ESQUIRE, SHERIFF.

N. B.—Those Prisoners who can both Write and Read are distinguished by *W. R.*—Read only *R.*—Cannot Read *N.*

No. Name, Age, Trade, &c.	Offence.	Sentence, &c.
1. EDWARD WEBBER 35, *Labourer.*—*W. R.*	COMMITTED 24th July, 1834, by J. M. LEAKE and T. NUNN, Esqrs. charged on the oaths of Robert Hardy and others, on suspicion of having, on the evening of the 10th or the morning of the 11th day of December, 1831, feloniously set fire to a certain stack, barns, and other premises, the property of the said Robert Hardy, at Tendring.	*DEATH recorded & reprieved*
2. WILLIAM WHEAL 27, *Labourer.*—*N.*	Committed 2nd August, 1834, by B. HARVEY, Clk. charged on the oath of George Coleman, with having committed an unnatural offence with a cow, at Blackmore.	*DEATH recorded & reprieved*
3. GEORGE RISBY 43, *Labourer.*—*W.R.*	Committed 7th August, 1834, by W. CODD, Esq. Coroner, charged with the wilful murder of John Spooner, at West Bergholt.	*Acquitted, being insane—to be kept in strict custody until His Majesty's pleasure be known*

71 View of Chelmsford from Springfield Hill by J. Colkett, 1847. The railway line, introduced four years before, can be clearly seen. On the extreme right is a man standing beside the track with a flag. The town still presents a very rural aspect.

72 Chelmsford railway station, *c.*1900. This building was erected in 1856 to cater for extra travellers to the Royal Agricultural Show of that year and replaced a wooden structure of 1843. It was to be replaced in the late 1980s by the rather more prosaic building still in use.

73 The *Black Boy Inn*, *c*.1852, formerly the *Crown*, the *New* and the *Queen's Arms* (later the *King's Arms*), where Cosmo de Medici stayed in 1669. It was demolished in 1857, leaving a gap in the High Street until the erection of *Barnard's Temperance Hotel* in 1868.

74 The Chelmsford Institute, built in 1841 at the cost of £2,500. The Literary and Mechanics Institute moved into the building in 1843, and by 1852 had over eight hundred members. Declining interest, however, led to its closure in 1899. The building, but for its façade, was demolished in 1975.

brickwork. The overall development included five other new streets: George Street, Writtle Lane (New Writtle Street), Bridge Road (Upper Bridge Road), Lower Anchor Street and Queen Street. The new accommodation, together with houses at Railway Street, Railway Square and Townfield Street which were built in the wake of the new railway, among others allowed for the sharp increase in population in the 19th century.

75 The Congregational Church, New London Road, erected in 1840 to the design of James Fenton, now the site of Allders. It had spaces for over 1,500 worshippers. The building was demolished in 1971, a year after its congregation and that of Baddow Road Congregational Church joined together in a new building further up New London Road.

76 Ebenezer Strict Baptist Church, New London Road, designed by James Fenton and built 1847–8. Like many other buildings in this part of New London Road, Friar's Place, Moulsham Street, Baddow Road and part of the High Street, it was subject to flooding in, for example, 1888 and 1947.

77 Chelmsford and Essex Hospital, New London Road was opened in 1883 by the Countess of Warwick. Several buildings nearby were used by the hospital, including Bellefield, former home of Frederic Chancellor.

78 The impressive façade of the hospital. Within the porch are tablets remembering benefactors such as George Wakeling, Thomas Cheveley and the Ridley family. £1,100 came from 'A Friend per St Mary's Offertory'.

Later in the century, the Essex and Chelmsford Infirmary and Dispensary was founded at the town end of New London Road. It was built by the subscriptions of local people, notably Arthur Pryor of Hylands, who laid the foundation stone. The hospital superseded the Chelmsford Free Dispensary, established in 1818 for the poor and also supported by subscription. It had moved from a site behind the parish church to New Bridge Street, then to Moulsham Street before its committee and volunteer doctors decided to appeal to the population to provide improved facilities. The new hospital was opened in 1883

by the Countess of Warwick. The facilities at this hospital and St John's Hospital in Wood Street were gradually moved from the 1990s to the growing regional hospital at Broomfield, originally established as an isolation hospital for tuberculosis sufferers in the 1930s.

The New London Road runs parallel with the old road to London, Moulsham Street, where buildings had been erected in a ribbon development over many centuries, as shown on the Walker map. Whilst the new properties had space and light and stood each side of a wide thoroughfare, many other properties in the town in New Street, Wood Street,

79 Moulsham Street near Baddow Road corner, *c.*1900, showing a mixture of ancient and, at the time, modern.

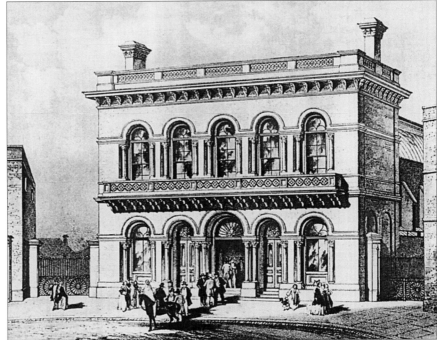

80 Chelmsford Corn Exchange, 1857, a building used not only for agricultural trade but also for entertainment for over one hundred years. It witnessed shows, dancing and such aesthetic pursuits as professional wrestling before demolition in 1969.

81 A not untypical shop at 65 High Street, *c.*1890. A large array of lamps is available and spades lurk in the doorway to the left. The owner of the shop Basil Harrison (left) stands with Alderman A. Morton. The shop was demolished in 1972 and Marks & Spencer now occupies the site.

82 The High Street, *c.*1910. A flock of sheep passes the Conduit, with the *Queen's Head* on the left and *Barnard's Temperance Hotel* on the right, the site of the *Black Boy*. A liveried coachman waits in front of the hotel and other conveyances can be seen in the middle ground.

83 Alderman Frederic Chancellor, 1825-1918, first mayor of the Borough and seven times mayor. He was a Fellow of both the Architects' and Surveyors' Institutes, county councillor, founder member of the Essex Archaeological Society, Lieutenant-Colonel in 2nd Volunteer Battalion, Essex Regiment and Freeman of Chelmsford. The *Essex Chronicle* said of him, 'He never wearied in well-doing'.

Rainsford End and parts of Moulsham were in very poor condition, and the absence of an adequate drainage system was a danger to the inhabitants. In 1831 a temporary Board of Health was set up to report on conditions. Its conclusions were dire. There were comments such as 'an accumulation of filth … and … putrid effluvia', 'everything about the house and its inmates exceedingly offensive' and 'the general appearance of the families on this spot induces your committee to think that disease is likely to arise'. They were prophetic for, in 1832, 21 cases of cholera were reported in Chelmsford, of which 11 were fatal. In 1848, there were 88 cases of typhus, of which six were fatal, and 25 cases of smallpox, three of which were fatal. The General Board of Health Inspector reported in 1849: 'To enumerate the bad and unhealthy conditions in the several dwelling-houses at Chelmsford would be to enumerate a very large proportion of the entire number.' In 1851, the residential population of the High Street alone was almost 700 and, according to the 1848 *Directory* of Chelmsford, the street was well paved and lit with gas. However, it was clear that some governing body for the town, enabled to make and enforce greater decisions for the benefit of the whole community, was needed.

The Public Health Act of 1848 gave the General Board of Health, a body set up by the Act, the power to appoint local boards, which could be established on receipt of a petition of one-tenth of ratepayers and following an inspector's report. A flavour of the inspector's report is given above. It followed a detailed tour of the town by the superintending inspector, Edward Creasey, who recommended that the Act should be applied to Chelmsford 'at once'. A public meeting at the Shire Hall in July 1848 led to an application being lodged to begin the process of setting up a local board. The application was successful and the new Board had its first meeting in September 1850. In the same year the Board appointed James Fenton, who was one of the Chelmsford Company members, as engineer and surveyor and charged him to make proposals on sewage and water matters. They also enacted new by-laws which *inter alia* outlawed the dumping of rubbish in public places. Fenton's report led the Board, in 1852, to provide sewers for the whole of Chelmsford and Moulsham. They also approved the creation of two reservoirs near the Burgess Well, behind what is now

the Civic Centre, and in upper Wood Street to supply water to support the sewerage proposals.

The Board consisted of 18 members including, for the first three years of its existence, the rector, Carew A. St John Mildmay, as Chairman. On his resignation he was replaced, in 1853, by John Copland, a member of the Company, who remained in the chair for 15 years. A new member in 1854 was Frederic Chancellor, already mentioned above. He had applied only three years earlier for the post secured by James Fenton and in 1858 he resigned from the Board to take up the job from which Fenton now resigned. In his new position, Chancellor was able to report that Fenton's work on the deodorisation of sewage at Lady Lane with an outfall down-river had been successfully completed. This work had been essential because the discharge of raw sewage into the Chelmer at Kings Head Meadow had led to an accumulation of solids, with the resultant pollution and smell. Subsequently, work by Chancellor saw the pumping of sewage to Barnes Farm through an iron pipe laid by the Board.

Whilst the Board was determined to provide safe water and adequate sewage disposal, they put considerable effort into the enforcement of rules on fire safety and building construction. New by-laws required builders, of whom many were at this time engaged in speculative building, to submit plans of proposed dwellings. These regulations applied also to commercial and other premises, including industrial sites. The Board forced unwilling traders to stop obstructing pavements and they also improved thoroughfares.

Frederic Chancellor resigned as surveyor in 1864, to be succeeded by Charles Pertwee, who was to serve until his retirement in 1887.

84 The Mayoral Chain and Badge, designed by Frederic Chancellor, and presented in 1889 by Henry Collings Wells. It is made in 18- and 22-carat gold with enamelling and platinum embellishments. There is also a Mayoress' Chain and Badge, the former presented by Miss M.F. Chancellor and the latter by Alderman T.J.D. Cramphorn.

85 The Borough Mace presented in 1889 by Charles Ernest Ridley. Made in silver, it weighs about 140 ounces and has, on the head, two shields enamelled in colours on 18-carat gold, one having the Royal Arms and the other the Borough Arms with the motto: 'Many Minds One Heart'.

Pertwee fulfilled the suggestion of his predecessor (regarding the provision of a sufficiency of water for the town in the future), by proposing a reservoir in Hall Street, which would be supplied from an artesian well and the Burgess Well. The reservoir was in use in early 1868. Chelmsford was fortunate to have the services of three distinguished engineers in creating an excellent water and sewerage system and a Board which backed their proposals. Against the background of an increasing population, the Board was involved in school attendance, smoke prevention, appointing a Medical Officer of Health and agreeing to the route of telegraph poles. They also considered the conversion, from gas to electricity, of street lighting.

But there were matters which a Board of Health could not undertake, such as the provision of a library. Among suggestions in 1886 for the celebration, in 1887, of the Golden Jubilee of Queen Victoria was the proposal that the town should be incorporated. The suggestion was not carried forward until the following year, when a public meeting was held at the Corn Exchange. By a large majority, the motion for incorporation was carried and an 18-member committee was established. A petition was started and an application made to the Privy Council, which instituted an Inquiry at the Shire Hall in February 1888. The need for a titular head of the town after the death in 1878 of the leading light in public affairs, Carew A. St John Mildmay, had been keenly felt and it was considered that only a mayor could fulfil this function. Incorporation might also bring benefits for trade and industry and quell the underlying fear of the mooted county authority. At first Frederic Chancellor had not favoured incorporation but he was persuaded that the majority of Chelmsford's inhabitants backed the move. Accordingly he swung behind the measure and the new borough was created, its charter being sealed on 7 September 1888.

The charter was brought by train from London to a town decked with flags and bunting. Temporary electric light was specially provided for the celebrations. A mile-long procession wound its way through the town, ending at the Corn Exchange where the charter was read by acting Town Clerk, Arthur Furbank, who had been a staunch supporter of

86   The Borough Coat of Arms, 1888-1974. The crossed crosiers mark the connection of the See of London and Abbey of Westminster with Chelmsford and Moulsham, the two elements at the time of incorporation. The bridge represents Bishop Maurice's bridge of 1100 and the lions rampant recall the arms of the Mildmay family and their association with the town.

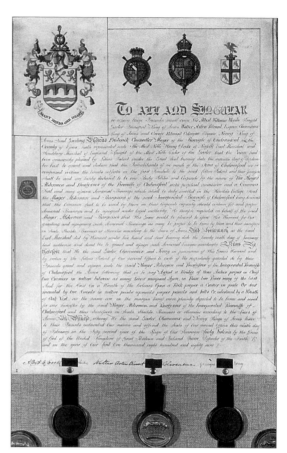

87   The Borough Charter dated 7 September 1888, which established two wards – North and South – and provided for six aldermen and 18 councillors. It was brought to Chelmsford by train on 19 September and read to a large crowd at the Corn Exchange by the acting Town Clerk, Arthur Furbank. The town was specially lit by electric light for the occasion.

incorporation. In November the first council elections were held and a new Council formed. The Borough's Arms were decided and the motto chosen: Many Minds – One Heart.

Earlier in the century, Thomas Wright had looked at the town from a sanitised perspective: 'The principal street, called High Street, … is wide and commodious' and 'the continual flow of water along channels on the sides of the streets carrying away all impurities keeps the town remarkably clean.' Others, too, were willing to overlook any faults to promote the

town, and in 1857 the Royal Agricultural Show was held on Durrants Field. Many societies were founded, including the Chelmsford & Essex Florist and Horticultural Society, whose gathering at the Shire Hall in 1824 was 'patronised by a considerable number of the gentry of the neighbourhood as well as of the town'. In 1828 the Chelmsford Philosophical Society was formed and, by 1835, was ready to start its own museum. One of its chief adherents was the Secretary, T.C. Neale, who, as Governor of the county gaol, gave the use of his parlour at the

88 A scroll showing the mayors of Chelmsford up to 1957, including Frederic Chancellor, Frederick Spalding, Thomas J. D. Cramphorn and John Ockelford Thompson.

89 Thomas Clarkson Neale, Governor of the County Gaol and first Secretary of the Chelmsford Philosophical Society and Chelmsford Museum. He made the first donation to the museum and supported it throughout his life. When he died in 1862 his daughter presented his collection of fossils.

gaol for the museum's first display space, though it is not known whether this was in the old gaol at Moulsham or the new one at Springfield. The museum moved to a new building in Museum Terrace in New London Road in 1843. Early exhibits were often bizarre: the skull of Robert Wright, executed at Chelmsford in March 1785; a prepared arm and an artificial snake; a dried frog and 'a curious old boot' said to have belonged to Charles II. Archaeology was not viewed with quite the same scientific rigour as it is today. A letter accompanying a

donation of Roman pottery from Wilderspool said, 'If you do not think these deserving of a place in Chelmsford Museum, pray dispose of them as you think best. They would make excellent drainage for flowerpots.'

The museum had its problems during the century but did hold many lectures and other functions at the Shire Hall. In 1880 there were musical and scientific soirées, which presented such marvels as Darby's Patent Pedestrian Digger, Edison's Talking Telephones and a phonometer, described as 'talking a hole

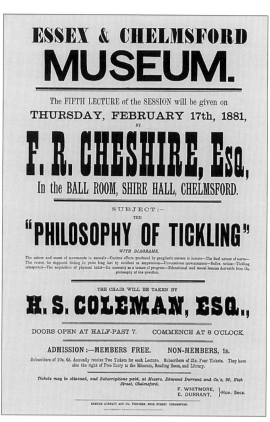

90 John Disney, 1779-1857, was a barrister and collector of antiquities. He was a long-term supporter of the museum in Chelmsford. He presented sculptures to the Fitzwilliam Museum, Cambridge which still form the core of their ancient sculpture collection. He also endowed a Chair of Archaeology at Cambridge, the first in Britain.

91 Museum poster: The Philosophy of Tickling. The lecture included reference to 'the ganglionic masses in insects' and 'Tickling interpreted'. With diagrams, this must have been a riveting evening.

through a plank'! Lectures included 'Early Man or Our Rude Forefathers', 'Animals with more than Two Eyes' and 'The Philosophy of Tickling', which tackled, amongst other things, the ganglionic masses in insects with diagrams. Most importantly, perhaps, the museum promoted the Cambridge extra-mural lectures, which helped bring more women into higher education. Unfortunately, by the end of the century it was closed and its objects packed away, some to be lost forever. Its revival came in the following century.

The *Essex Review* of 1892 named a number of other societies then in existence: the

Chelmsford Musical Society, the Chelmsford Association of Church Choirs, the Chelmsford Philharmonic Society, the Chelmsford Pianoforte and Vocal Clubs and the Private Society for the Practice of Strict Glee and Part-Song Music (unaccompanied). The *Review's* founder and proprietor was Edmund Durrant, a wholesale stationer and bookseller, then at 90 High Street. He was Secretary of the museum for some years and arranged the Cambridge University lectures. In 1888, he formed the Chelmsford Odde Volumes, later termed 'a bookish club of genial eccentrics', to encourage interest in fine arts, music, archaeology and science. Its members lectured each other on their own special interest or outside speakers were invited. In 1892 Professor W.R. May talked on 'Some Records of the Rocks', Rev. T.L.Papillon, Vicar of Writtle, took 'The State and Secondary Education' as his subject, while George Day related his experiences in Paris during the Prussian siege of 1870/71, including his comments on eating donkey, cat and rat. The Rev. W.L. Benthall lectured on 'Egypt – Past and Present, illustrated with a series of beautiful lantern views'. Each member was elected to the 'Shelf' and then given an unique volume number. Edmund Durrant was Volume I. The Treasurer was known as Honorary Cash Book and the Secretary as Honorary Minute Book and each volume would answer only to his volume number or title, not his proper name. Meetings were held on the 'accustomed shelf', that is 90 High Street. A 'Ladyes' set was formed in 1896 but the society outlived its founder and mainstay by only four years. Durrant died in August 1900.

Chelmsfordians pursued sporting activities too. For example, the West Essex Bicycle Club was formed in 1875 with its headquarters at the *Saracen's Head*. The first county meet of cyclists was in Chelmsford in 1879. In 1878 the Chelmsford Lawn Tennis and Croquet Club was founded, and in the following year the Chelmsford Cricket Club was reformed, the first recorded game having been in 1755. In 1893, Lord Rayleigh was the first President of the newly formed Chelmsford Golf Club, and the Chelmsford Hockey Club started in 1898. There were also sporting activities associated with local factories. A prime mover in football and athletics was Robert Cook, Secretary of the West Essex Bicycle Club and organiser of the county meet mentioned above

and also secretary of the Essex Football Association for 23 years. He founded the County Sports Meeting in 1885. His election to the Borough Council in 1906 was followed by his death in 1908.

Apart from the erection of whole new streets, many new buildings were erected during the century. By 1828 the new County Goal at Springfield was completed with Thomas Clarkson Neale as its Governor. Work had begun in 1825 and prisoners were moved there as wings were completed. St John's Church was opened in 1836 to give the hamlet of Moulsham its first established church. In 1857, to complement the Royal Agricultural Show, the new Corn Exchange was erected to the Italianate design of Frederic Chancellor. Subsequently, in 1880, the whole market was removed from the High Street to an area behind the Corn Exchange, thus freeing the street from the weekly mess caused by livestock and traders, though cattle and sheep continued to be driven through the town until after the Second World War.

The movement of the market was a boon to the proprietors of shops, inns and other businesses in the High Street. For centuries they had been forced to accept the pens set up at the head of the street and the movement of all manner of livestock with the concomitant refuse, filth and inconvenience. Frederick Spalding, recorder of daily life of Chelmsford through the many photographs he left of the town in the late 19th and early 20th centuries, recalled in a talk at the YMCA hut in 1930 that,

> It was not by any means a rare thing for cattle to stray into shops. On one occasion, while my premises were in Tindal Square, a young bull belonging to Lord Rayleigh not only came in on the ground floor but mounted two storeys of the house ... A great deal of damage was done ... He

92 Museum Poster: A Grand Scientific and Musical Soirée. Such events were a mixture of modern science, such as 'the phonomotor (talking a hole through a plank)', music, performance and exhibitions. They were often held at the Shire Hall and were well attended. Admission was one shilling for members and two shillings and sixpence for others.

93 Odde Volume Number One: Edmund Durrant, described by the *Weekly News* as 'that best of good-natured fellows'. One of the Odde Volumes' trips was to the pottery at Castle Hedingham, where Durrant was captured in clay. According to one obituary, he was 'respected and revered by all classes'.

entered a sitting room on the first floor and a bedroom (occupied by two lady assistants) on the second floor. Fortunately they were away at the time. Perhaps he wanted his photograph taken. We were so anxious to get him downstairs – I quite forgot to ask him to give me a sitting.

The market was owned by the Mildmay family but, after significant public pressure, in 1875 the local Board of Health decided to buy rather than lease the market and remove it from the street. It was purchased for £2,000

and an area was earmarked behind the Corn Exchange and the Grammar School, the approximate modern site of High Chelmer and the multi-storey car-park down to the River Can, and a new road cut from Duke Street in a dog's leg, then called Market Road, now Market Road and part of Victoria Road South.

Another of the former responsibilities of the manor was removed in 1842 when the Constables Act awarded to the parish vestry

94 The Crompton Arc Works Rugby XV, 1892-3. From left to right: (Top) G.H. Jackson, A.L. Stevens, R.B. Roberts, W.S. Entwistle, – Grey, A.B. Randall, E.E Hankinson, A.S. Palmer. (Middle) J.S. Hamilton, R.B.J. Binnie, G.M. Clark, J. Christie. (Bottom) R.E. Perry, H.A. Neale, H.B. Price. Like Hoffman's, Marconi's, Clarkson's and Christy's, Crompton's provided sporting and other social activities for its employees. A race meeting in August 1911, including all the above firms, was held at the Wood Street Grounds, now the site of Tesco's, Princes Road.

95 The gravestone of Robert Cook (1858–1908), at the Borough Cemetery, Writtle Road, which depicts his sporting interests and remembers his enthusiastic support and promotion of them for the benefit of all. His tombstone calls him 'The pioneer of Essex Athletics'.

the election of local constables. They were to come under the authority of the first Chief Constable of Essex, Captain John McHardy, who had his police headquarters in Old Court in Arbour Lane. McHardy had had a lively naval career, notably in the West Indies, and been Inspecting Commander of the Coast Guard before taking up his police appointment. Before he died in 1882, he achieved the rank of Admiral.

96 HM Prison, Chelmsford as shown in a postcard of the late 19th century. The incised words 'County Gaol' can just be seen over the door; previously it was inscribed 'Convict Gaol'. Completed in 1828 for 272 prisoners, the prison needed extensive re-building after a fire in 1978.

97 The impressive façade of the Corn Exchange, *c.*1900. Judge Tindal's statue looks up Duke Street past the *Golden Lion* public house. The people have probably been asked to remain still to avoid fuzziness in the photograph. Here even the dog has stayed at rest!

98 Chelmsford Market was always a busy town centre attraction with its mixture of livestock sales and commercial sellers. Here is the scene when the market was behind the Corn Exchange, now the site of Chancellor Hall.

Another change, but one which did not have much of an effect on the general populace, came as the result of the pressure applied by the Bishop of London, Charles J. Blomfield (1828-56). He urged the Ecclesiastical Commissioners to transfer Essex and most of Hertfordshire from London to the Diocese of Rochester. This was achieved by an Act of 1845 and ended the association of the London Diocese with the town which had started in the seventh century. In 1877 the

new See of St Albans was created covering both Essex and Hertfordshire, but it was not until the new century that Chelmsford itself would be created a diocese.

The *Essex Business Review* of 1888/90 noted the importance of Chelmsford's agricultural trade: 'Chelmsford is ... chiefly known as an important agricultural centre; while the industries of the place are almost entirely such as have a more or less direct bearing upon farming.' The *Review* did, however, look to the

99 Chelmsford Market, *c.*1900. Cattle wait in the street to be sold. The selling area is to the left. Joslins, Agricultural Engineers, on the right, have a plough and harrow displayed on the pavement in front of the shop.

future: 'The trades centred here are conducted in an able manner and every effort is made to develop existing industries and create new ones.' It is true that the town had industrial concerns such as the Coleman and Moreton, established by Frederick Greenwood in 1843, which was very successful for some time in supplying ploughs, cultivators and other agricultural equipment. They also made steam engines including engines for a steam ploughing system, castings for bridges and manhole covers, and wrought iron work. Their factory on the south side of New London Road, called the London Road Iron Works, was on the corner of New Writtle Street. It suffered from the agricultural depression of the late 19th century and foundered, the site being sold in 1907. Another

business, producing traction engines, portable steam engines and land-digging equipment, which succumbed to the depression was that of Eddingtons, set up in 1856 in Springfield Road, moving to New Street/Victoria Road (the present police station) in 1859. In 1871 the partners were William and Sylvanus Eddington and they employed over fifty men and boys. Others, like Christy, which was established in 1858 by Fell Christy and his father James as a mill-wrighting concern, expanded, becoming Christy & Norris by 1897 and manufacturing machinery for the food and agricultural industries. Another family company, Christy Brothers, moved into electrical engineering.

In his reminiscences of 1900, Edmund Durrant said,

100 The High Street from an illustration in the *Essex Business Review* of 1888/9. The *Review* noted that, 'The population at present reaches about 11,000 ... [The town] is well paved and lighted and possesses many handsome and elegant shops, some of which are rather extensive, in a provincial sense.'

101 The *Half Moon Inn*, junction of the High Street and New London Road, in pencil and Conté by A. Bragg. Next door is the butcher's shop of Albert Nokes. It was said that the longest journey in the world was between the *Half Moon* and the *Rising Sun*, another public house at the top of Moulsham Street/New London Road.

102   Crompton's Arc Works in Writtle Road, now the site of the 'Village' redevelopment. The first Arc Electric Works were established in Anchor Street in 1878. These premises suffered a major fire in 1895 and Crompton erected a purpose-built factory here to replace them. The factory closed in 1969.

The granting of the Charter in September 1888 is no doubt the best event that has happened in the town's history. The increase in trade since the Charter has been remarkable. The Arc Works have largely extended, Messrs Hoffman's ball-bearing have been erected and last, but not least, the Wireless Telegraphy Manufactury has brought a unique trade among us. No doubt other industries will quickly follow were it not for the difficulty of getting dwelling houses for the work people.

The industries which Durrant mentions had, for the first time, no direct connection with the town's agricultural past. Indeed they all looked to the future. Colonel R.E.B. Crompton had come to Chelmsford in 1876 as a partner in the firm of T.H.P. Dennis. It was his interest in electric arc lighting which led to the founding of Crompton & Company Electrical Engineers in 1878 and the establishment of a firm which became one of the most important manufacturers of electrical equipment in Britain. It also provided many jobs for the town's working population for almost a hundred years.

The Hoffman Manufacturing Company was established in 1898 and it, too, became a major employer. It retained the name of the patentee of the precision steel balls it made, Ernest Gustav Hoffmann, though he was bought out, early in the new century, by Charles and Geoffrey Barrett. The third of the new type of industrial business was Marconi's Wireless

103 Hoffmann's new works on the corner of New Street and Rectory Lane. The four-storey buildings which remain are now used as offices and flats but the factory buildings, closed in 1988, were demolished and the site has now been occupied and developed by Anglia Polytechnic University.

Telegraph Company Limited. Guglielmo Marconi set up the first radio factory in the world in Chelmsford in 1899 and the first purpose-built radio factory in the world in 1912 which he was to develop into a major world-class concern in the 20th century. From small beginnings, Marconi was to be a principal employer in the town, who, unlike Crompton and Hoffmann, was to survive throughout the 20th century and into the 21st. Fluctuation in

104 A blue plaque, sited in Mildmay Road, marking the establishment of 'the first Radio Factory in the world'. Marconi chose a former silk factory in Hall Street/Mildmay Road for his works. The site is now the premises of Essex & Suffolk Water PLC.

world markets and injudicious management policy have, however, almost led to its demise at the beginning of the new century.

The loss of older firms echoing the importance of local endeavour and the establishment of the new industries reflected the changes which were to overtake Britain in the 20th century, particularly after the Second World War. For a number of reasons the town had expanded: the coming of the railway and the canal coupled with agricultural depression led to the transmogrification of many people from agricultural to factory workers. The town was also the seat of the new county administration.

105 The Recreation Ground or 'Rec', *c*.1900, opened in 1894 through the subscriptions of local people. The lake was excavated in 1842 to provide earth for the railway viaduct. Laid out with flower-beds, paths and seats, it saw the celebration of festivities such as the Coronation of George V in June 1911. The 'Rec' was later split by the building of Parkway.

Five

The Modern Age

But with the chequered Past you'll find
The glorious present intertwined, …
Sir Gurney Benham on the Golden Jubilee of the Borough in 1938

Chelmsford entered the 20th century as a fledgling borough. It left it with serious aspirations to the status of a city. In 1999 the town's Chief Executive, Martin Eastall, said, 'The Council will make the best possible case for Chelmsford that we can … for the town to be made a city either at the change of the millennium or the 50th anniversary of the

Queen's accession in 2002.' The bookmakers, William Hill, clearly thought at the time that Chelmsford's case was the strongest in Essex, giving Southend on Sea 28 to 1, Colchester 25 to 1 and the county town 16 to 1. The perennial rivalry between Chelmsford and Colchester was commented upon in 'Essex Leaders' in 1906:

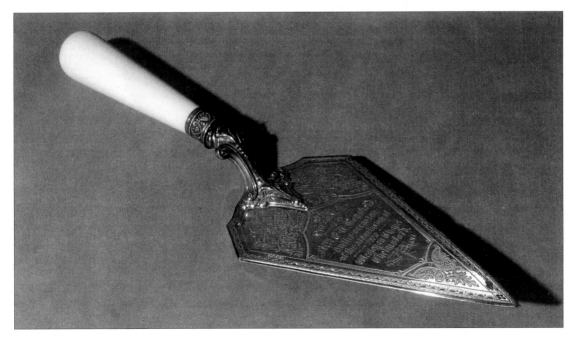

106 A silver presentation trowel presented to Mrs G. Bonsfield on the occasion of her laying the foundation stone of the Wesleyan Church on 2 June 1897.

107   The Wesleyan Church opened in 1898 on the site of the modern Cater House. The church could hold 800 worshippers with an additional 400 seats for children in the attached Sunday School. The buildings were said to have suffered from inadequate piling of the riverside.

The claims of Colchester to be considered the more progressive town of the two and a town offering the best facilities for the discharge of County business have often been urged by the citizens of the Oyster Borough. In view, however, of Chelmsford's record of public works and its present progressiveness – the keen municipal spirit which has been awakened by the activities and independence of its public men – these claims can be set aside with little compunction.

In 1903, the town honoured Field Marshal Sir Evelyn Wood with the first award of the Freedom of the Town, another mark of the borough's establishment.

In 1901 the population of the borough was 12,627 and by 1921 it was 20,769. The estimated population after the Second World War was 33,500. The borough boundaries were extended in 1897, 1907 and 1934. The expansion of the town was due to a combination of factors: proximity to London; communications by road, rail and, at least until 1927 when coal ceased to be brought in by barge, by canal; the introduction of new industries such as Thomas Clarkson's steam bus

108 'The Changing Face' in mixed media by John Thornton Bell, showing the building of Cater House in 1960–1.

manufactory; the county's increasing administrative involvement in the town, and the effects of the agricultural depression which witnessed the move of many from the countryside to the urban environment. After the Second World War, people moved from the capital to escape burgeoning traffic and pollution and ageing inner-city housing. New towns such as Harlow and Basildon attracted many Londoners, but Chelmsford and other Essex towns also saw immigration from this source.

On 25 May 1898, a Wesleyan Chapel was opened in the High Street next to the Stone Bridge. It was reported that 'Messrs Kite & Co. London, have supplied the hot water apparatus by which the buildings are warmed.

The electric light supplied by Messrs Christy Bros of Chelmsford is quite a feature and has so far proved successful.' The building was demolished in 1971 to make way for one of Chelmsford's few tower blocks, Cater House, in which was opened one of the town's first supermarkets.

In 1900 Edmund Durrant died and the town lost one of its most important leaders. His efforts in promoting the library and museum were not in vain, however, and in 1906 both institutions were brought together in a building in Market Road, now Victoria Road South, which was also to house the School of Art. The building was to the design of Frederic Chancellor (and indeed was later

109 An informal group which includes, seated right, Alderman Fred Spalding, who was a councillor for 54 years, including three as mayor. He was made a Freeman of the Borough in 1933. We are indebted to him for his many photographs of the town from the late 19th and early 20th centuries.

110 The building in Tindal Square where Fred Spalding had his shop and studio, seen at the very top. The *Essex Business Review* noted that he had a 'flourishing trade in fancy goods, bags and useful articles … his establishment will at any time repay a visit'. He later moved to a shop in the High Street.

to be called the Frederic Chancellor building), who waived his fee. Part of the cost was borne by the American industrialist and philanthropist, Andrew Carnegie, who was only prepared to support the library element of the project. When Lord Rayleigh laid the foundation stone in 1904, he urged that 'the ratepayers' money should not be spent on too lavish provision of sensational fiction for the library … men should read not merely for

111 The Public Library, Museum and School of Art, Market Road (now Victoria Road South), *c.*1906. The museum moved in 1930 and the library in 1936 and the building was later known as the Mid Essex Technical College and School of Art, the precursor of Anglia Polytechnic University. The Baptist Church next door was opened in 1909.

112 Chelmsford swimming pool in Waterloo Lane opened in May 1906.

113 The monogram of Edward VII (1901-10), from an original drawing by Derek Wilks, on the former Post Office building at No. 1 High Street.

114 Duke Street 1882, from a watercolour by W. Brown. The part of Duke Street from Broomfield Road to the railway was formerly called King Street. Until they were demolished in 1875, a row of cottages stood on the Civic Centre site.

relaxation but at times when they have their wits about them.'

Also in 1906 an open-air swimming pool was opened in May in Waterloo Lane. It had 'an open dressing shed, 80 feet in length. Thirty-six dressing boxes provide ample accommodation for bathers and there is a cycle shed. The work of construction, which has occupied about nine months, has cost nearly £700.' Hot slipper baths were added in 1914 and an indoor pool was opened in August 1965. An extended complex named Riverside Ice & Leisure was opened in 1987. It incorporated both the swimming pools and a new ice rink plus fitness rooms and other amenities.

The sum of societies in the town was augmented in 1910, when Lady Pretyman, wife of the local Member of Parliament, opened the Conservative and Unionist Working Men's Club in the former Post Office in the High

Street, 'which has been altered and adapted to suit the needs of the members, who at present number 280'. These premises became available when a new Post Office was erected and opened in 1908 at No.1, High Street. Four royal ciphers of Edward VII can still be seen on the building, including two on the hopper heads, which channel water from gutters to down-pipes.

Directly next to the Post Office was Barclay's Bank, built after the demolition in 1905 of Frederic Chancellor's house. Barclay's had merged with Sparrow Tufnell & Co. in 1896 and provided banking services at the start of the century in competition with the Westminster, formerly the London, County & Westminster. (Chancellor moved to Bellefield in New London Road, where he died in January 1918, shortly after being awarded the Freedom of Chelmsford.) The erection of the new premises for the bank is an indication of the growing prosperity of the town at the time.

In 1903, the National Steam Car Company began to manufacture steam buses in its Clarkson Works premises in Lower Anchor Street, next to Crompton's old Arc Works, off Moulsham Street. The National Omnibus Company operated locally from 1913 from the present bus garages in Duke Street, then King Street. The Company purchased the premises in 1918 and by 1930 Eastern National was established in the town. Before the First World War steam vehicles, petrol-driven motors and horse traffic co-existed on busy but not over-crowded streets.

The Marconi Company erected the first purpose-built radio factory in the world in New Street in 1912. It was built at great speed, being completed in 17 weeks, and employed some 500 men. The first publicised

115 The Marconi Factory, New Street was built in 17 weeks in 1912 by 500 workers. It was the world's first purpose-built radio factory and Britain's first official radio broadcast, by the Australian singer Dame Nellie Melba, was made from here in June 1920.

entertainment broadcast in Britain was transmitted from New Street in June 1920, and in 1922 the first licensed regular broadcasting station was established at Writtle. The hut from which the broadcasts were made is preserved by Chelmsford Museum. The New Street Factory was also used for the development of picture transmission and television transmitters were designed and made there. The factory was almost opposite the ball-bearing manufactory of the Hoffmann Manufacturing Co., and New Street was packed with pedestrians, cyclists and buses at certain periods every day. Both companies were vital for war production, and in the Second World War were targets for enemy bombers.

116   The Marconi Factory, New Street showing the 450-foot high masts which were erected in 1912 and were a landmark for 20 years before demolition in 1935. In the foreground are railway sidings. A line ran across New Street so that incoming and outgoing goods could easily be transported by train.

Hoffmann's expanded its production during the century to become the largest employer in the borough. It became part of Ransome Hoffmann Pollard in 1962 but was closed and the machinery and land sold off in 1988. The site is currently occupied by Anglia Polytechnic University. Similarly, Cromptons suffered closure in 1969 although one department remained until 1982 in New London Road under the name Hawker Siddeley. Crompton had merged in 1927 with F.& A. Parkinson to form Crompton Parkinson and their site in Writtle Road expanded incrementally during the century. It is now the home of 'The Village' housing complex.

For many years Chelmsford had a military presence. In 1859 the Armoury and Depot of the West Essex Militia was established in the area off Moulsham Street known as Barrack Square, now the site of Chelmsford Star Co-operative Stores. The Depot moved in 1879 to the Headquarters of the Essex Regiment at Warley, Brentwood, but in 1903 Earl Roberts of Kandahar opened a new Drill Hall off Market Road for the peace-time equipment and drill of volunteer units. The town saw a large influx of troops in August 1914, men of the strategic reserve held in towns in the eastern counties against enemy invasion. King George V visited Chelmsford in October 1914 to inspect 15,000 men in training at Hylands Park. The presence of troops affected even the Beef-Steak Club. In August and September, 'no room was available for the monthly meeting of the Club, the whole of the Saracen's Head being in the occupation of the H.Q. of the South Midland Division'. In January 1920, 'as a result of the war … the price paid by each member for the monthly dinner was raised from 5s. to 6s. 6d.'.

Recruitment of men for war-time services left gaps in the workforces of local firms and women moved to fill the void. Both Oaklands House and Hylands House were used as hospitals for wounded troops and the homes of local families were used as billets for soldiers who remained in the town until the war ended.

In 1914 the parish church became a cathedral when the Diocese of Chelmsford was formed to serve the geographical county. The 1913 Bishoprics of Sheffield, Chelmsford and for the County of Suffolk Act gave to the new See 'the County of Essex and that part of the County of Kent which lies north of the River Thames'. The church building was originally dedicated to St Mary. In 1954, on the 1300th anniversary of the conversion

117   A Crompton Parkinson long-service badge for 25 years' service. In 1927, Crompton & Company merged with F. & A. Parkinson of Guiseley to form Crompton Parkinson Ltd.

118   The main offices of Crompton Parkinson in Writtle Road being adapted as part of the comprehensive redevelopment of the site by Fairview in 2003. The present building was finished in 1919, a remodelling of the original 1896 office.

119 A card issued by Fred Spalding to commemorate the wedding of Claude Grahame-White and Dorothy Taylor of New York. Grahame-White was anxious to promote the use of aircraft and arrived for his wedding by aeroplane. The wedding became known as Britain's first aero wedding. Unhappily it ended in divorce.

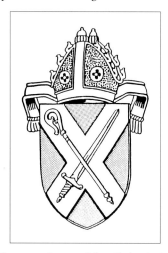

120 The coat of arms of the Chelmsford Diocese. It combines the sword from the Arms of London diocese with the saltire of Rochester and the field has the colour of the golden saltire of St Albans. It is the second largest diocese in England, with a population of about three million.

of the East Saxons to Christianity by St Cedd, the dedication was extended to include St Cedd and St Peter, for whom St Cedd's seventh-century church at Bradwell on Sea was named. The figure of St Peter, dressed as a modern fisherman and holding a Yale type key, executed by T.B. Huxley-Jones, can be seen in the south-east corner of the South Chapel. Improvements and alterations to the cathedral were made during the century, including the embellishment of the South Porch as a memorial to the airmen of the United States Air Force who were stationed in Essex between 1942 and 1945. Among the stained glass in the porch are representations of the great seal of USA and of US Air Force insignia.

121 The figure of St Peter by T.B. Huxley-Jones on the south-east corner of the South Chapel of the cathedral, facing towards the ancient church of St Peter at Bradwell. From an original drawing by Derek Wilks.

Although plans were drawn up in 1920 by Sir Charles Nicholson for significant extensions, including a new nave and choir, these were never built. In 1983, however, drastic refurbishment and re-ordering was carried out which, among other things, saw the removal of the traditional pews in favour of chairs, to give flexibility to the space within the church. A new pulpit was set up, in bronze and steel to the design of Guiseppe Lund, and dubbed locally 'Boudicca's Chariot'. The installation of a new limestone floor and under-floor heating gave the opportunity for archaeological examination of the area. In 1994, a new organ, the first in an English Anglican cathedral for more than thirty years, was installed by N.P. Mander Ltd. Made by hand, it has four manuals and pedals and forty stops. It has 2,600 pipes ranging in size from ¾inch to 16 feet.

In his book *Highways and Byways of Essex* of 1939, Clifford Bax declared that 'an artist, an antiquary or a humanist will not find much in

122 Interior of the Cathedral, *c*.1914. The pews were removed during alterations in 1983 and new seating introduced to give 'flexibility for worship as well as for musical events, particularly the annual Chelmsford Cathedral Festival in May'. A second organ, in the chancel, was installed in 1995.

Chelmsford to excite him but the place must have dismal or delightful associations for many a curate, commercial traveller or barrister. The Chelmer does what it can to alleviate the comfortable dullness of its offspring but, for once in a way, even water is unable to produce beauty.' Bax clearly did not appreciate the more mundane advantages of the town. In April 1935, for example, the Library, together with a civic suite comprising Mayor's Parlour and committee rooms, was opened in Duke Street on the site of Fairfield Lodge. In 1938, Chelmsford City became a professional football team with a new stadium in New Writtle Street. The Chelmsford Races at Galleywood still attracted large crowds to the twice-yearly two-day meetings in the 1920s and 1930s.

A new bus station opened in 1931 and was extended in 1937. In 1933, the foundation stone to County Hall was laid. A nine-storey tower block and two three-storey buildings were completed in May 1965. Moulsham Schools were officially opened in September 1938 by the mayor, Councillor J. T. Bellamy, on part of the site of Moulsham Hall lands. The schools comprised infants, juniors and seniors on a single campus. The Education Committee's official programme noted that 'strict economy, consistent with sound building, has been observed throughout and all unnecessary ornamentation has been avoided'. However, 'the rooms and halls are wired to plugs for cleaning and wireless installation'.

In 1930, the Chelmsford & Essex Museum moved from Market Road to Oaklands House in the newly-acquired Oaklands Park. There had been disagreement in the Council about the museum moving there. Councillor W.A. Leach said, 'Have we really definitely decided to use this "white elephant" as a museum? It seems to me that the Library Committee has

... gone stark, staring mad in the way of expenditure.' Nevertheless, the museum did move, and on the day of the opening of the park and museum to the public an anonymous poem was written which began:

> The Mayor and Lady Mayoress they had a golden key,
> So let us go to Oaklands Park, and ope it wide said he.
> Oh yes she cried that will be fine and on this great occasion
> I'll get the band to play some tunes, you bring the Corporation.

It ends:

> The spacious grounds about the house which form the Oaklands Park
> Will be open to the public all day until nearly dark.
> The Museum and the pictures will all be open free
> With close at hand a splendid place where one can get some tea.
> But if, when wearied with the games, as the sun sinks down in glory
> The Rising Sun's across the way – but that's another story.

Two years later the museum was visited by Prince George, fourth son of George V. The Prince also paid a visit in May 1932 to view the County Fayre and Social Services Exhibition. He went to the Marconi Telegraph Company, where he was received by 'his Excellency Marchese Marconi'. He had lunch at the Hoffmann Manufacturing Company and took tea at Crompton Parkinson Ltd. His principal engagement, however, was to open a new bypass, called Princes Road, on which Moulsham Schools were to be sited. Work on the 3¼-mile bypass, with bridges over the Chelmer and the LNER railway line, had begun in September 1930 and cost £200,000. It was, as the *Essex Chronicle* described it, 'part of a big scheme for a ring road completely round the Borough'. An advertising feature around the report on the opening mentioned the new *Army and Navy* public house, 'a superb

123 Oaklands House and Park. Originally the area was part of the manor held by the Abbot of Westminster. The house was erected *c.*1866 for Alderman Frederick Wells, a local brewer and coal and timber merchant, and acquired by the Council in 1930. The Essex Regiment Museum was opened by HRH The Princess Margaret in 1973.

new Temple of Bacchus', 'a different kind of inn – every endeavour will be made in this attractive road house to meet the requirements of the travelling public'.

Prince George had not, however, come to Chelmsford by road or rail. He had piloted himself to Broomfield aerodrome, where he was greeted by the Lord Lieutenant of the County, Brigadier R. B. Colvin, who had officially opened the aerodrome on 18 May. At the opening, Sir Alan Cobham and his Air

Circus had been guests. Sir Alan commented, 'We are trying to see that every town and village has its own aerodrome ... With aerodromes everywhere, aeroplanes will become as common as cars.' Fortunately, he was wrong.

The bypass helped to ease congestion in the town centre, particularly on market days when livestock were still driven through the streets. Mr Cyril Yarker, recording his reminiscences for the museum in the 1980s, remembered another aspect of one market day: '... a large

124   The *Cross Keys*, Moulsham Street before demolition and the erection of the Regent Theatre. From the middle of the 17th to the beginning of the 19th centuries the site was used as the county gaol. From a watercolour by Alfred Bennett Bamford.

crowd turned up and, after waiting patiently in the dark, a conveyance arrived with the apparatus. Soon a large white sheet covered the wall of a cattle shed … and we were gazing on the first pictures that we had ever seen …'. Mr Yarker recalled this being before the first cinema opened in the town, the Empire Picture House in Springfield Road. The cinema had seating for 524 and survived until 1940, when a severe fire prevented further use for cinema purposes. It had opened in about 1912, the same year the Select, later the Select Kinema, was set up in New Writtle Street. In 1953, the Select was the first cinema in Essex capable of showing Cinemascope films.

Ten years later, however, it was a bingo hall, reverting in 1988 to cinema presentations. It closed in 1992, and in 1993 became a Laser Adventure Megazone.

The Regent was erected in 1913 on the site of the 15th-century *Cross Keys Inn* in Moulsham Street. Originally it was for theatre performances but showed films from August 1916. It seated 1,086 people and had stage facilities and dressing rooms. It was used for both functions until after the Second World War. In 1975 it became a bingo hall, but by the 1990s, and despite protests, it was converted for use as the Chicago Rock Café. In 1920, the Pavilion Super Cinema was opened in Duke Street,

125 The Pavilion Cinema in Duke Street in the 1950s. Next door is Denoons, the main Ford dealer. In the foreground is an unashamed cigarette advertisement.

126   The Odeon Cinema, Baddow Road in 1966. It is now the site of a multi-storey car-park.

becoming simply the Pavilion in the 1930s. Its capacity was 500. It closed in 1988 and was subsequently altered to house Laser Quest and later Zeus, a nightclub.

Perhaps Chelmsford's grandest cinema, the Ritz, was opened in 1935 to the design of Robert Cromie and had 1,748 seats plus a restaurant and ballroom. These became popular venues in their own right. The children's shows on Saturdays were remembered in the town long after the cinema had disappeared. It was renamed the Odeon in 1947 and continued under that name until its closure in 1981, then demolished eight years later having lain derelict during that time. Its name lives on in a multiplex, sited only yards away from the origi-

nal, which was opened in 1993 with four screens.

As the world moved towards the Second World War, Chelmsford was a prosperous, if congested, town with a regular market day, entertainments and a bypass. Its shops included the department store of J.G. Bond, Boots the Chemists and, by 1938, according to the *South-Eastern Counties of England Trades' Directory*, two television repair shops, Flexmans of Duke Street and W.H. Smith's in New London Road. Both were also listed as Wireless Engineers. Whilst these were in the van of progress, more traditional establishments listed were ten smiths, seven saddlers, two rope makers and five 'Registry Offices (Agencies) For Servants'.

127 Carnival procession in Duke Street in the 1930s. The annual Chelmsford & Essex Hospital Carnival began in 1923 and Fred Spalding was chairman of its committee for several years.

128 F.G. Keen, Chelmsford Auxiliary Fire Service, from an original oil painting by Bernard Hailstone. Leading Fireman Frederick Keen was awarded the OBE for his bravery at an oil installation during an air raid.

Wenley Ltd and Bolingbroke & Sons were then separate establishments, only joining together in 1967 and finally closing their joint enterprise, well known to all local people, in 2000. They were joined in their demise in 2003 by J.H. Clarke & Co. Ltd, once the town's premier bookshop and artist's suppliers.

In the early days of the war, Chelmsford Borough and its Rural District received evacuees, including children and pregnant women, some of whom were housed at Danbury Park. Road signs were removed and

129   Civil Defence personnel practising at the Corn Exchange.

defensive measures taken. 'Dragon's Teeth', pyramid-shaped concrete blocks used as tank traps, were laid and were still extant in places after the turn of the millennium, as were pill-boxes in Little Waltham and Springfield. Hundreds of air-raid shelters were built, many in the area of the Hoffmann and Marconi works in New Street and Rectory Lane. In September 1940, during the Battle of Britain, many locals saw a dog-fight over the town. Some bombs were jettisoned and minor damage was done to Chelmsford Golf Course in Widford. A wartime rule of the Club stated: 'A ball moved by enemy action may be replaced as near as possible to where it lay or, if lost or destroyed, a new ball dropped not nearer to the hole without penalty'.

Because of its industrial importance, having as it did the Hoffmann, Crompton and Marconi works each making its contribution to the war

130 Commemorative garden, Borough Cemetery, to 36 employees of the Hoffmann Manufacturing Company, killed in 1942 and 1944. The memorial was re-dedicated in October 2002 after refurbishment.

effort, Chelmsford was a significant enemy target. In early May 1941 the Marconi factory was bombed. Seventeen were killed and 20 seriously hurt. Production was badly affected. Hoffmann was hit in July 1942 when seven were killed. Five hundred properties were badly damaged. Despite the establishment of a balloon barrage at over thirty sites in the town in October 1942 and a Home Guard Rocket Anti-Aircraft Battery, largely manned by local factory workers, in the Recreation Ground in August of the same year, another air raid on 19 October killed four Hoffmann workers, seriously injured six and hurt a further fifty-nine. In neighbouring Henry Road five were killed, including a ten-year-old boy, David

Westrip. Hoffmann's worst attack, however, took place on 19 December 1944, when a V2 rocket fell on the factory, killing twenty-nine. These, and earlier casualties are remembered in a small commemorative garden at the Borough Cemetery in Writtle Road. The same rocket killed nine people in Henry Road.

Chelmsford suffered many other casualties. In the 5 May 1941 air raid, besides the Marconi casualties, six were killed in Coval Lane. In the heaviest raid of the war, on 14 May 1943, 50 residents were killed, over 3,000 properties were damaged and hundreds were made homeless. There was considerable damage in Victoria Crescent and Townfield Street and, at the bus garage, 13 buses were destroyed.

Also affected were Victoria Road, Lower Anchor Street, Upper Bridge Road, Baddow Road and Lady Lane. Eleven elderly people were killed at the New Hall Emergency Hospital at Boreham.

On the 15th of the previous month, an incendiary raid affected Broomfield and Springfield. Twenty-eight fires were reported, including one at HM Prison in Springfield Road, where the stores and the Governor's House were burnt out and everything lost. It was noted in the Director's Minute Book that the effects of the incendiaries would have been much worse but for the efforts of the Governor, staff and prisoners. A major fire at the Cathedral was also averted through the actions of three teenage fire guards who extinguished a fire caused by a bomb.

Apart from conventional raids, damage was caused by V1 and V2 rockets. The first local V1 hit Boreham Aerodrome on 16 June 1944 and others subsequently fell at Ingatestone, Galleywood, Sandon, Rettendon, West Hanningfield and at the Chelmsford Swimming Pool, which was partly demolished. In addition to the V2 which caused such tragic loss of life in December 1944, others fell at Runwell, Broomfield, Writtle, Bicknacre, Ramsden Heath and Woodham Ferrers.

The first enemy missile to fall from the sky was not a bomb, however. On 19 June 1940, a Heinkel He III landed in the garden of the Bishop of Chelmsford at Bishops Court in Springfield Road, having been shot down by FO 'Sailor' Malan, DFC. In another incident, a Spitfire of 19 Squadron, flown by Sub-Lt. Arthur Blake, was shot down, crashing into Oak Lodge, New London Road, opposite Oaklands Park. The pilot was killed. The first civilian casualties were on 19 August 1940 in Gainsborough Crescent. Two women and a

girl were killed by a bomb probably aimed at the Police Headquarters at the north-west end of the crescent. The best-known casualty of the war was Alderman John Ockelford Thompson, CBE, DL, JP, who was killed when a bomb demolished his home, Brierly Place, New London Road on 13 October 1940. He was mayor of the town at the time and had held that office seven times. He was awarded the CBE in 1938 for his valued public services. His wife Emma was also killed, together with their son, Thomas, a member of their staff, Alice Emery, and their two grand-daughters of eight and 14 months.

The end of the war in Europe was celebrated on 8 May 1945 in Tindal Square, where there was dancing and singing. The King's speech was relayed to the crowds and thanksgiving services were held at the Cathedral at intervals throughout the day. In the evening there were bonfires and AA lights were turned skywards. Similar celebrations were held on 15 August to mark the end of the war in the Far East. An open-air service of thanksgiving was held on the steps of the Corn Exchange on 19 August led by ministers of various faiths in the town. Chelmsford Gramophone Society celebrated too, on 25 September, at their monthly meeting at the Mid Essex Technical College in Market Road, when their President, F.W.F. Hendry presented a programme entitled 'Music For Victory'.

The end of the war also saw the first General Election since November 1935. The death, in December 1944, of the Member of Parliament for Chelmsford, Colonel John Macnamara, brought a by-election in April 1945 which was won by Wing Commander Ernest Millington of the Common Wealth Party, a left-wing grouping. At the General Election in July 1945, Millington was supported by the

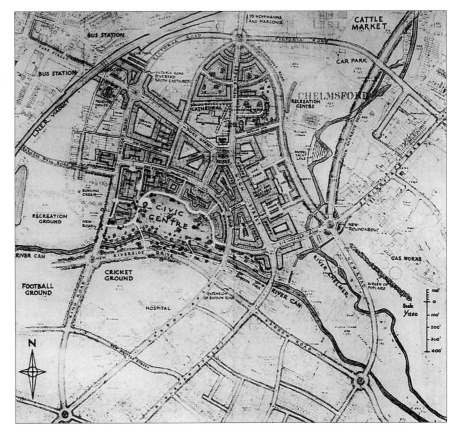

131 Chelmsford Planning Survey 1945: The Centre Replanned. The plan shows a new Riverside Drive, a new road joining Market Road (Victoria Road South), a Civic Centre and concert hall.

Labour, Communist and Co-operative parties and retained his seat with a majority of over 2,000. In April 1946, he joined the Labour Party.

Before the end of the war, a group named the Chelmsford Area Planning Group, which had been formed in 1935 by a number of residents of both the Borough and Rural District, organised an unofficial survey of Chelmsford and its surroundings. It was supported by Hoffmann, Marconi and Crompton Parkinson and had the co-operation of both Councils. With the help of 200 voluntary workers, the Group, under the direction of Anthony Minoprio, MA, FRIBA, AMTPI produced a report including 30 survey maps and ten drawings. In May 1945, an exhibition of its findings and suggestions was mounted at the Shire Hall and opened by Professor Sir Patrick Abercrombie. It was visited by over 3,000 people.

The report opened: 'The need for re-planning in Chelmsford is patent to all', but later stated that 'There can be few towns in England that offer so great an opportunity for good planning, for the two rivers have preserved the centre of the town from overbuilding.' Its six conclusions were that the town had a bad road plan; central area land was wastefully used; architecture and amenities were poor; the Can and the Chelmer were neglected; there was a deficiency of houses and public buildings and the residential areas lacked the amenities they should have. Yet Chelmsford was 'the industrialised centre of one of the five most important administrative

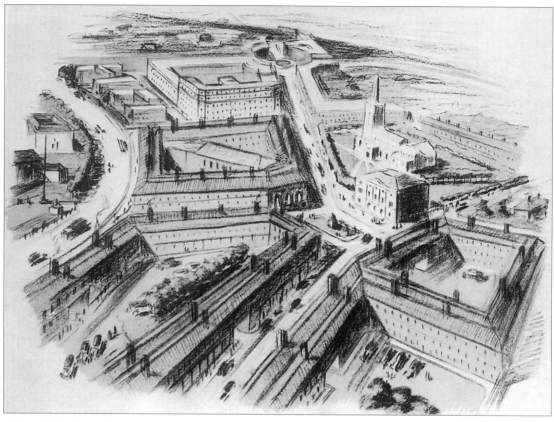

132   Chelmsford Planning Survey 1945: The High Street and Tindal Square. Whilst the Shire Hall and Cathedral remain the same, the rest of the centre of the town has lost its interesting roof lines and individuality.

counties in England'. The main recommendation of the Group sought to ensure close co-operation in the future between town planner, architect, engineer, surveyor, medical and education officers and, interestingly, sociologist. Other recommendations and suggestions were grouped under roads, rail and bus services, cattle market, town centre, residential areas, public services, open spaces and architecture and amenities. Many of the suggestions were gradually taken up by the Council who, fortunately, did not follow the Group's grand design for the town centre, which appeared to be influenced in some ways by small town America. They did, however, remove traffic from the High Street, build an inner relief

road, increase car-parking, move the cattle market, develop the Can and the Chelmer and build residential areas as self-contained units, although some of these developments took many years to be realised.

In the design of new council estates, the self-contained principle was followed at, for example, Westlands or Meadgate, where shopping areas supplied more than just the immediate needs of residents. The Council's *Town Guide* of 1973 indicated that, in the 20 years following the cessation of hostilities, 4,599 dwellings had been erected. Melbourne Park was built between 1946-8 with additions in 1952-3, Chignal in 1951, Woodhouse between 1949-50, Springfield Park from 1946-51 and

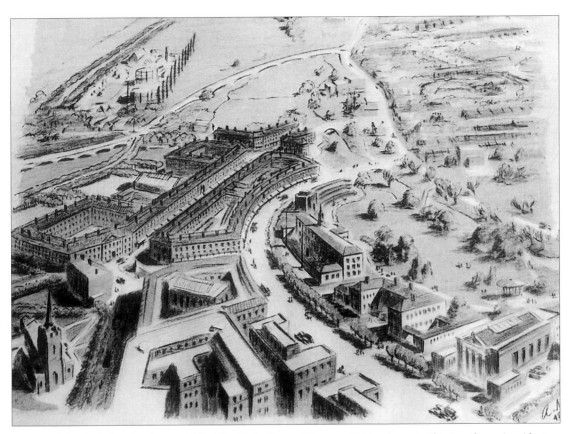

133   Chelmsford Planning Survey 1945: The Civic Centre. The monolithic, almost totalitarian, theme is evident.

others at Westlands, Waterhouse Lane, Upper Bridge Road, Baker Street, Arbour Lane and Meadgate. In 2001, after a poll of council property residents, it was agreed that the housing stock should be transferred to a housing association, in line with the extensive development of private estates, particularly in Springfield in the 1980s and 1990s, at Chelmer Village and elsewhere, in accordance with government decrees requiring a minimum number of houses. Such developments attracted the attention of shopping chains which used land away from the main retail area. Firms such as B&Q, Comet, Halfords, Asda and Sainsbury's sought to offer free parking, easy family access and a wide choice of goods as an inducement to shop with them. By the end of the century, Chelmsford's shopping centre had to vie with out-of-town stores and with shopping complexes at Lakeside, Grays, Bluewater in Kent and Freeport at Braintree.

In 1972 High Chelmer shopping precinct was opened, welcomed by many since it brought large firms such as C&A, Sainsbury's and W.H.Smith to an undercover, traffic-free environment. Others bemoaned the loss of the Corn Exchange and the destruction of Tindal Street (formerly Conduit Street or Back Street), which lost its western side, including shops and public houses, to blank walls and service yards. In 1954 Sir Nikolaus Pevsner said of Chelmsford:

> A walk through the town does not afford much excitement. But it is pleasant, because the centre

134 Chelmsford Planning Survey 1945: The Town Hall and New Tindal Street. Nothing of the old street remains, having been replaced by the appearance of the mid-western United States.

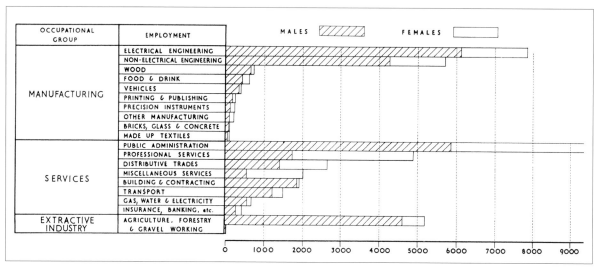

135 Employment Structure in Chelmsford 1949, from the County of Essex Development Plan 1952. The bar chart reflects the three main strands of employment in engineering, administration and agriculture. Fifty years later much of the first had disappeared.

136   New London Road, 1966, showing the buildings to be demolished for the erection of the High Chelmer shopping precinct. On the left is Museum Terrace, built in 1843 and occupied by the museum until 1899.

has remained singularly unaffected by the coarser and louder forms of commercialisation. The main streets are still architecturally quiet and in scale with the Shire Hall and the former parish church. The High Street has little in the way of individually remarkable houses. The best is No.26 with its centre window with brick pilasters carrying Corinthian capitals of stone and a brick pediment, early Georgian probably. Opposite three varieties of modern: The Dutch, the quiet 1950, and the Tecton-Fry-International – all three in provincial dress.

Two decades later, the Meadows shopping centre was developed to give a second major precinct joined by a now pedestrianised High Street. Such developments had the beneficial effect, amongst other things, of maintaining the town's healthy employment record, despite the loss of previously large employers such as

Hoffmann and Crompton Parkinson and the diminution of work at Marconi.

Along with residential and retail developments went a programme of public buildings and works. In December 1951, Sir John Ruggles-Brise opened the Melbourne Park Festival Pavilion to celebrate the Festival of Britain. In the early 1960s, a flood relief scheme canalised the rivers within ugly concrete walls, successfully preventing the recurrence of the perennial flooding of parts of the High Street, Moulsham Street, Baddow Road, Friars Place and New London Road.

In May 1962, a civic hall, the Civic Theatre, was erected as an all-purpose venue. It was not until 1973-4 that the Council committed the

137 The corner of Tindal Street, 1966. Wainrights café, Cramphorn's seed shop and the *Dolphin* public house are visible in the foreground, with the Corn Exchange in the right background. All these premises were demolished in 1968/9 and the area now has a blank wall and a service yard.

138 The Mansion House, 26 High Street, was built in 1754/5 for Dr Benjamin Pugh. It was used for some time as the lodging of the Assize Judge, when he sat at Chelmsford. From an original drawing by Derek Wilks.

building to exclusive theatre use by raking the floor as part of a refurbishment programme. This had become possible because of the inclusion in High Chelmer of the Chancellor Hall, set over the main Post Office and close to the Corn Exchange, which had been demolished in 1969. The Hall proved to be a mixed blessing and was never a very popular entertainment venue. It became, to many, the

Council's 'white elephant'. The opening, by telephone from South Africa by Chancellor's granddaughter, was marred somewhat by a flood in the gentlemen's toilet. A plea for accommodation for musical events had been made as early as 1893:

> Is it too much to hope for that Chelmsford will some day have a concert room worthy of the County Town? The ballroom at the Shire Hall is for many reasons inadequate for anything like a concert on a large scale. The Corn Exchange is very bad acoustically and anything but comfortable … Will some of the leading men of the Borough take the matter up?

Chancellor Hall was not the answer but the Council has taken up the challenge. The theatre was developed next to the Library in Fairfield Road, whilst the Duke Street frontage was augmented by the Civic Centre building, opened at the same time and sometimes referred to by locals as being built in 'early chronic' style.

To make way for the High Chelmer, or C.D.A. 15 as it was unromantically known, the Cattle Market was moved to a site in Victoria Road purchased in 1948 and opened by Christopher Soames, Minister for Agriculture, Fisheries and Food in June 1963. Access to the area may have been helped by the opening of the first stage of the inner relief road, Parkway, in July 1967. Towards the end of the century the market moved again, this time to a new area at Springfield. It was by the saddest coincidence that it closed virtually in the same year as the celebrations for the grant of the original market charter.

In 1966 the Council purchased Hylands Park, Writtle, and opened it in May of that year to allow residents the chance to walk in the lovely grounds of a mansion previously owned by Mrs Christine Hanbury, who was connected with the brewers Truman, Hanbury

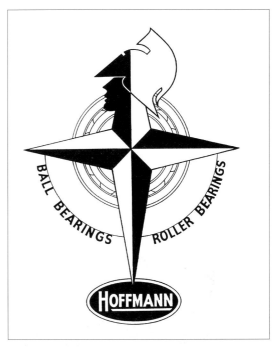

139 Advertisement for Hoffmann's from a Festival of Britain 1951 souvenir programme. The mayor, Arthur Andrews, in his introduction, said, 'We are endeavouring in a very modest way to participate … a little more gaiety than is normal will go a long way … [to] banish austerity …'.

140 Festival of Britain 1951: an advertisement for fashion. Arthur Andrews said, 'Let us do all we can to put a little sunshine, which has been so long absent during the winter of 1950-51, now happily only a memory, into the lives of our youngsters.'

141 Fairfield Road 1966. Beyond the Civic Theatre, erected four years before, the road is still residential. Subsequently the houses were demolished and the Cramphorn Theatre, 1982, and further council offices were built.

and Buxton. The grounds were bought to enable the Council to reach the standards recommended by the Physical Training and Recreation Act of 1937 but the somewhat dilapidated house came too and, until the 1980s, the use of the house gave great concern to councillors, who knew that any access to it from the A12 trunk road was unacceptable to the Ministry of Transport. Many suggestions were investigated but turned down, and in 1975 the Council decided on demolition, so a Public Enquiry was held in 1976. Permission to demolish was refused and later a disposal

brief was drawn up to attract those who might wish to develop the house alone. It had deteriorated further due to the theft of roofing lead and to dry and wet rot. By 1985 none of the suggested uses, which included a casino and hotel and luxury flats, had come to fruition and the Council decided to restore the building to its early 19th-century form. Work began in 1986 with the aid of a grant from English Heritage. The house was opened to the public in May 1995 and further work on restoring the interior has been carried out to enable rooms to be used for weddings and other

142 Rainsford House and War Memorial. Rainsford House was converted in 1924 to accommodate the Borough Council's offices. It was demolished to make way for the opening of the Civic Centre in 1962. The War Memorial was erected in 1923.

143 Friars School, Friars Place, established in 1840 by the British and Foreign School Society. It closed in 1960 and was demolished in the late 1960s to make way for the second stage of Parkway.

events. The park itself has been well maintained and, with the exception of the proposal for a golf course within the grounds which, to the relief of most, did not proceed, the Council has varied the use of the park from time to time to attract new visitors.

One of the suggested uses for the house had been as a museum. This was costed and fully

144 Hylands House, *c.*1770. Built *c.*1730 for Sir John Comyns, once Chief Baron of the Exchequer and MP for Maldon, in Queen Anne style, the house was extended and enlarged in the 19th century by a series of owners. Many millions have been spent in restoring it to its early 19th-century appearance.

145 V98 Music Festival in Hylands Park. Virgin established these concerts in 1996 and they have become one of the premier such festivals in Britain, attracting thousands of visitors each year.

146 Duke Street, *c*.1900. Being the main thoroughfare from the town centre to the railway station, it was always busy. Basil Harrison, in *A Duke Street Childhood* said, 'From butchers to bootmakers, gardeners to grooms, mantle makers to medical practitioners and cutlers to confectioners, all lived and worked in Duke Street.' From a watercolour by Alfred Bennett Bamford.

considered, but it did not go forward. However, in April 1973, after much work on recording and transferring exhibits to a Regimental Trust, and on the design of a new structure and new displays, the Essex Regiment Museum, formerly at Warley Barracks, Brentwood, was opened by HRH The Princess Margaret at Oaklands Park, part of the Chelmsford & Essex Museum. This air-conditioned, windowless extension was variously dubbed a

cigar box, an air-raid shelter or a public loo. It proved extremely popular and the staff have answered many queries on the regiment and its members over its two hundred years of service.

Following the Redcliffe-Maude Report, the Borough and Rural District Councils were amalgamated in 1974 and some functions of the former Borough were transferred to the County Council, such as the library service.

147 County Hall, showing the juxtaposition of the old and the new: the 1930s meet the 1980s.

The new District Council was headed, not by a mayor, but by a Chairman. In 1975 new armorial bearings were granted to the enlarged authority as a borough and the office of mayor was restored.

Chelmsford Prison suffered a major fire in 1978. A muffled blast was heard before a conflagration which cost an estimated £1 million and required the evacuation of all 218 prisoners, who were sent to Pentonville and Wandsworth Prisons. Before inmates were returned to the rebuilt structure, permission was given for a feature film to be made there, based upon the very popular television series *Porridge*.

In the 1970s, Chelmsford's unsought notoriety as a traffic black-spot worsened, particularly with regard to the Army and Navy roundabout, from which long traffic jams emanated each summer weekend as people made their way to the coasts of Essex, Suffolk and Norfolk. Local residents and travellers found some relief when, in 1978, a single-way flyover was built over the roundabout. It helped the traffic in and out of the town from the Southend direction but did little to address the major problem, which only a by-pass could solve. After considerable public consultation on the preferred routes, central or southern, it was decided to cut through open land to the

148 Chelmsford High Street, 2003. For over nine hundred years, the centre of the town's activities has been here and, although the furniture has changed, the layout remains the same.

south of the town and a new nine-mile stretch of the A12 opened in 1987. But a new generation of traffic problems still affects the town. Increasing use of the car suggests that this virtually insoluble problem will continue indefinitely.

The Cramphorn Theatre opened in 1982, a smaller venue than the Civic Theatre next door and designed for more specialist performances. The cost of the structure was met from the bequest of Alderman T.J.D. Cramphorn, six times mayor of Chelmsford, who left part of his estate to the Council in 1912 to provide a Town Hall or other building 'likely to advance the dignity of the County Town'. The

Chelmsford Theatre Association considers that 'Chelmsford now has a theatre complex in which it can take pride'.

The centenary of the Borough's existence was celebrated in 1988 with a whole pro- gramme of events including the Annual Museum Lecture (Hilda Grieve on The Apprenticeship of a Borough), concerts, sports events, Prunella Scales (An Evening with Queen Victoria), a Charter Ceremony and Mayor's Ball. At the end of July, HM The Queen visited the town for the third time, to open the new County Hall complex and Central Library. The year also saw the publication of *Chelmsford Celebrates*, an illustrated, light-hearted

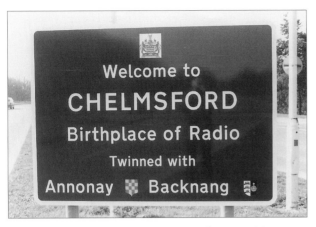

149 The proud signs now welcoming visitors to the county town to celebrate the town's international importance and its valued associations.

booklet looking at the town's past and present, which included a short history of the town and souvenir calendar of events. One of the principal events was the Chelmsford Centenary Spectacular held at Hylands Park in late August, the first of a series of spectaculars stretching into the new century. At the first Spectacular, there was a full-scale Civil War battle, the RAF Battle of Britain Memorial Flight, the Band of the Royal Engineers, the Royal Philharmonic Pops Orchestra, Humphrey Lyttelton, Helen Shapiro and Alan Price, plus crafts, rallies, exhibitions and workshops.

In 1982, the Conservatives lost power in the council chamber for the first time in many years to the Liberal Democrats. Control has changed back and forth in recent years. The turn of the century brought the replacement of local democracy by the introduction of the cabinet style of administration dictated by central government.

In 1987, much of southern England was devastated by the worst storm for 300 years. Hylands and Oaklands Parks suffered badly, the latter losing an ancient Turkey Oak specimen. Many trees were blown down and

traffic was severely affected. Almost as bad as this natural catastrophe, though not nearly as important, was the verbal onslaught on Chelmsford by Gavin Stamp, writing in the *Independent* in March 1989 under the heading 'Exceptionally Mediocre'. Mr Stamp savaged the town and found particular delight in rounding on the Cathedral authorities for their treatment of the church's interior.

But space by the rivers was opened up and new businesses were established in the town centre, many for the young such as Dukes, Zeus, Edwards and Yates Wine Lodge. In a survey of 1,100 town centres in November 1998, Chelmsford was placed forty-third and both local papers commented: 'The best town centre shopping in Essex' said one and, in a rather more English manner, 'Another survey says Chelmsford is rather good.' In October, the *Chelmsford Weekly News* carried a piece about litter in the town under the headline 'Dirty in 1935; Still dirty now says reader'. The following week the *Essex Chronicle* quoted the local Member of Parliament, Simon Burns, under a counter-attacking and quite awful headline: 'M.P. slams dirty town rap'.

In 1990 Chelmsford was twinned with Backnang, near Stuttgart in southern Germany, and is now also twinned with Annonay, France and Bacsalmas, Hungary. The Chelmsford Cathedral Festival brought varied and quality programmes to the Cathedral and other venues for music, art and lectures. In 1998 the town celebrated again, this time the 900th anniversary of the beginnings of the market.

In 2001/2 the Council mounted a campaign to make Chelmsford a city at the time of the Golden Jubilee of Queen Elizabeth. Despite very great efforts by the Council and private firms, the bid was unsuccessful, the town losing to Preston. The *Essex Chronicle*, however, used the disappointment to start a campaign promoting 'Pride in Chelmsford'. In the previous year the Council had erected road signs on the approach roads to the town indicating that Chelmsford was the 'Birthplace of Radio'. Though accurate and well-meaning, the timing was unfortunate since the Marconi Company was to suffer very badly in world markets and very considerable sums were wiped from its assets, resulting in redundancies in several parts of the world and anxious uncertainty for its many employees in Chelmsford.

In 1999 a body was created, intended to exist only for a year or two, which called itself Chelmsford Photo. 2000 or CP2K. It comprised members from the Friends of Chelmsford Museums, the Chelmsford Society, the Essex Society for Archaeology and History, the Chelmsford Association of Photographic Societies, the Museum and Essex Record Office. It set out to record photographically the town in its various aspects in the single millennial year. CP2K deposited the resulting 1,100 images in the Essex Record Office for digitisation and permanent access for the public. A subsequent well-researched and illustrated limited edition book entitled *Caught in Time: Chelmsford in Colour* was published and copies deposited at the Museum, Library and Essex Record Office. Despite the disappointing start to the new century, CP2K, under the chairmanship of the author, succeeded in providing for future Chelmsfordians a comprehensive picture of their town, thriving, buoyant, busy, a product of international and national trends and pressures but still the sum of its chequered past. The county town of Essex has every right to be proud of its heritage and to look to a bright, if crowded, future.

Bibliography

Abraham, E., *Hylands, An Architectural History*, 1988

Bax, Clifford, *Highways and Byways of Essex*, 1939

Begent, A.J., *Chelmsford at War: A chronicle of the county town of Essex during the Second World War*, 1999

Booker, J., *Essex and the Industrial Revolution*, 1974

Briggs, N., *John Johnson 1732-1814. Georgian Architect and County Surveyor of Essex*, 1991

Chelmsford Borough Council Minutes, *Chelmsford Celebrates*, 1988

Chelmsford Museum: *Local History Index; Minute Book of the Chelmsford Philosophical Society, 1828-54*

Chelmsford Photo. 2000, *Caught in Time: Chelmsford in Colour* 2002

Chelmsford Rural District Guide Commemorative Edition, 1973

Coller, D.W., *People's History of Essex*, 1861

Directories: Kelly's Directory; Pigot & Co. Directory; Post Office Directory 1874; Jewell's Directory 1922; South-Eastern Counties of England Trades' Directory 1938-9 40th Edition

Drury, P.J., *The mansio and other sites in the south eastern sector of Caesaromagus*, 1988

Edwards, A., *A History of Essex*, 5th Edition, 1994

Edwards, A. and Newton, K.C., *The Walkers of Hanningfield: Surveyors and Mapmakers Extraordinary*, 1984

Ellis, J., 'The Gentlemen who laid out London Street: Study of Housing and Development in S.W. Essex, 1839-51', Local History Dissertation, 1983

Essex Archaeological Society: *Transactions*

Essex Chronicle

Essex County Handbook: Official Guide to the County

Essex Journal

Essex Review

Essex Weekly News

Essex: Who and where 1909: A Muster Roll of Prominent Men and Women and Leading Residents in the County of Essex

Feather, Fred/Shepherd, Frank, *150 Years of Service: Essex Police 1840-1990*

Foreman, Stephen, *Hylands: The story of an Essex country house and its owners*, 2nd Edition, 1999

Frere, Sheppard, *History of the Provinces of the Roman Empire: Britannia*, 1967

Friends of Chelmsford Museums:

    Gone But Not Forgotten: Reminders of Vanished Chelmsford, 1996

    Pastimes in Times Past: Fun and Games in Chelmsford, 1999

    Chelmsford & Moulsham: An Historical Walking Guide (Jones, D.L. and Scarborough, J. with illustrations by Derek Wilks), 1999

Gaskill, W. and Press, C.A.M., *Essex Leaders Social and Political*, 1906

Grieve, H., Annual Museum Lecture 1988: 'The Apprenticeship of a Borough' (unpublished)

Grieve, H., *The Great Tide: The story of the 1953 flood disaster in Essex*, 1959

Grieve, H., *The Sleepers and The Shadows: a town, its people and its past*:

    Volume 1 *The Medieval and Tudor Story*, 1988

    Volume 2 *From Market Town to Chartered Borough*, 1994

Grimwood, Bob, *The Cinemas of Essex* (no date)

Hedges, J.D. and Buckley, D.G., *Springfield Cursus and the Cursus Problem*, 1981

Hedges, J.D. and Buckley D.G., *The Bronze Age and Saxon Settlements at Springfield Lyons, Essex. An interim report*, 1987

Hill, C., *The Century of Revolution 1603-1714*, 2nd edition, 1980

Hewitt, Canon G., *To Frame the Heart* (no date)

Hewitt, Canon G., *History of the Diocese of Chelmsford*, 1984

'History of the Incorporation of the Borough of Chelmsford 1899', reprinted from the *Essex Weekly News*

Hudson, Elleen, *The Lives and Wills of Essex Token Issuers Incorporating a Re-Listing of the Seventeenth Century Trade Tokens of Essex*, 1987

James, Prue (ed.), 'A Duke Street Boyhood: Growing up in Chelmsford, 1900-1918' by Basil Harrison, 2001

Jarvis, S.M., *Chelmsford in Old Picture Postcards*, 3rd edition, 1990

Jarvis, S.M., *Essex: A County History*, 1993

Jarvis, S.M., *The World of Fred Spalding: Photographs of Essex 1860-1940* (Introduction), 1992

Jarvis, S.M., *Chelmsford: The Archive Photograph Series*, 1997

Kemp, K., 'The Urban Growth of Chelmsford and Moulsham 1591 to 1851', dissertation presented for the MA in Local and Regional History, Essex University, 1998

Kenyon, J.P., *Stuart England*, 1978

Marriage, John, *Chelmsford: A Pictorial History*, reprint 1988

Marriage, John, *Changing Chelmsford*, 1992

Marriage, John, *Chelmsford: Britain in Old Photographs*, 2nd edition, 1997

Marriage, John, *Barging into Chelmsford: The Chelmer and Blackwater Navigation*, 2nd edition, 1997

Marriage, John, *Chelmsford Past and Present*, 2000

Mason, A., *Stuart Essex on the Map*, 1990

Morant, Philip, *History and Antiquities of the County of Essex*, 1768

Morris, J. (ed.), *Domesday Book: Essex*, 1983

Muilman, Peter, *A New and Complete History of Essex … by a Gentleman*, Volume One, 1771

Origins of Chelmsford, Borough Council/Essex County Council, 2002

Norden, John, *Speculi Britanniae Pars: An Historical and Chorographical Description of the County of Essex*, 1594

Page, W. (ed.), *Victoria History of the County of Essex*, vol.1, 1903

Pevsner, N., *Essex: Buildings of England Series*, 1954, originally published by Penguin Books

Pledger, C.M., *History of Baddow Road Congregational Church*, 1968

Scollan, Maureen, *Sworn to Serve: Police in Essex 1840-1990*, 1993

Stenton, D.M., *English Society in the Middle Ages (1066-1307)*, 2nd edition, 1952

Thompson, R., *Around Chelmsford: Francis Frith's Photographic Memories*, 2001

Tildesley, Kate, Chelmsford Museum Founder's Day Lecture 2002: 'Kismet McHardy: Chelmsford People and the Sea'

Torry, G., *Chelmsford Through the Ages*, 1977

Torry, G., *Chelmsford Prison*, 1980

Torry, G., *The Book of Chelmsford*, 1985

Trevelyan, G.M., *English Social History*, 1944

True North Books, *Memories of Chelmsford*, 2000

Tuckwell, A., 'That honourable and gentlemanlike house': A History of King Eward VI Grammar School, Chelmsford 1551-2001, 2001

Tuffs, J. Elsdden, *Essex Coaching Days*, 1969

White, William, *History, Gazetteer and Directory of the County of Essex*, 1863

Wickenden, N.P., *Caesaromagus: A History and Description of Roman Chelmsford*, 1991

Wickenden, N.P., *The Temple and other sites in the north-eastern sector of Caesaromagus*, 1992

Wickenden, N.P., *A Brief History of Chelmsford at the Borough's Centenary*, 1988

Wickenden, N.P., *A Celebration of Chelmsford*, 1999

Wright, T., *History and Topography of the County of Essex*, Volume One, 1836

Index

References which relate to illustrations only are given in **bold**.

INDEX